PENGUIN BOOKS

SHAKESPEARE O

Born in Liverpool and ~~~~~~~~~~~~~, Michael Kerrigan is a freelance writer and journalist, reviewing regularly for *The Times Literary Supplement* and the *Scotsman*. His books include *Who Lies Where: A Guide to Famous Graves* (1995), *The Wit and Wisdom of Jane Austen* (1996) and the Penguin anthology *To Be or Not to Be: Shakespeare's Soliloquies* (2002). He now lives in Edinburgh.

Shakespeare on Love

Edited by Michael Kerrigan

PENGUIN BOOKS

PENGUIN BOOKS

Published by the Penguin Group
Penguin Books Ltd, 80 Strand, London WC2R ORL, England
Penguin Putnam Inc., 375 Hudson Street, New York, New York 10014, USA
Penguin Books Australia Ltd, 250 Camberwell Road, Camberwell, Victoria 3124, Australia
Penguin Books Canada Ltd, 10 Alcorn Avenue, Toronto, Ontario, Canada M4V 3B2
Penguin Books India (P) Ltd, 11 Community Centre, Panchsheel Park, New Delhi – 110 017, India
Penguin Books (NZ) Ltd, Cnr Rosedale and Airborne Roads, Albany, Auckland, New Zealand
Penguin Books (South Africa) (Pty) Ltd, 24 Sturdee Avenue, Rosebank 2196, South Africa

Penguin Books Ltd, Registered Offices: 80 Strand, London WC2R ORL, England

www.penguin.com

First published 2003
1

Introduction and editorial matter © Michael Kerrigan, 2003
All rights reserved

The moral right of the editor has been asserted

Set in 10.25/12.5 pt PostScript Monotype Dante
Typeset by Rowland Phototypesetting Ltd, Bury St Edmunds, Suffolk
Printed in England by Clays Ltd, St Ives plc

Contents

Introduction

Now no discourse, except it be of Love;
Now can I break my fast, dine, sup, and sleep,
Upon the very naked name of Love.   (II, iv, 137–9)

This little book takes up the challenge which Valentine throws down to himself in *Two Gentlemen of Verona*: love, as it is encountered in the works of Shakespeare, is its sole subject. Valentine's regime may sound monotonous, its ardour not so much sublime as obsessive, and there are indeed dissenting voices to be found among Shakespeare's own romantic characters. 'Love is merely a madness . . .' says a sceptical Rosalind to Orlando in *As You Like It* (III, ii, 384), yet her own story shows how much more there may be to love than she allows.

In fact, to read Shakespeare on love is to enjoy an endless variety and boundless delight. Even if, as has had to be the case here, such categories as familial love and friendship are ruthlessly excluded, that still leaves an enormous range of other sensations and sentiments, registers and moods. Romantic yearning, breathless passion, the dizzy distraction of the heart's first flutterings: all these feelings find expression in Shakespeare's plays and poems. There are other emotions too: the ache of disappointment, the pangs of separation and the pain of loss. 'The course of true love never did run smooth,' as

Lysander puts it in *A Midsummer Night's Dream* (I, i, 134). And, as so many of Shakespeare's characters find, love is by no means invariably 'true': here, too, then are the anguish of rejection, the frenzy of jealousy and the shock of betrayal.

Shakespeare writes with a certain authority: the author of some of the most moving love poems in the English language in the Sonnets, he created two of the world's most celebrated lovers in the 'star-crossed' Romeo and Juliet. Although they are not so famous as her 'O Romeo, Romeo!' speech, Juliet's reflections a little later in the 'Balcony Scene' are as entrancing an account of the wonder of love as any that we have:

My bounty is as boundless as the sea,
My love as deep. The more I give to thee,
The more I have, for both are infinite.   (II, ii, 134–6)

Fine words, yet they take a special poignancy from our awareness that she herself will prove only too tragically finite. Our sense that Romeo and Juliet are rushing headlong towards ecstatic extinction lends a dangerous excitement to a play in which erotic and dramatic drives are simultaneously sweeping us along. All the great speeches to be found in Shakespeare derive an extra dimension from their dramatic context – a dimension which is missing from a collection of this kind. Yet the plays themselves, in their 'two hours' traffic' (*Romeo and Juliet*, Prologue, 12), are inevitably impressionistic in their account of love. They literally have no time for all the ongoing ups and downs, the daily give and take of the sort of realistic relationships we may read about in novels, or, for that matter, experience ourselves. The narrative demands of the drama will, moreover, invariably impel events towards the sort of clear conclusion not generally to be found in real life, whether tragic death or the happy ending of the comedies. In this respect, the works of Shakespeare prove remarkably well suited to this sort of selection, delineating as they do an idea of love whose overall complexity finds expression in a momentary insight here, a grand declaration there, a tender thought or an agonized outpouring somewhere else.

Even so, the dramatic context of any passage always has to be borne in mind, if only for the ironic texture it may lend. Take, for example, the verses in Hamlet's *billet doux* to Ophelia (II, ii):

Doubt thou the stars are fire.
   Doubt that the sun doth move.
Doubt truth to be a liar.
   But never doubt I love.   (II, ii, 115–18)

These lines, conventional though they are, allow us to imagine another dramatic vocation for the eloquent Prince: the philosophical soliloquy's gain may have been the romantic lyric's loss. Yet how does Hamlet's love for Ophelia, expressed so unreservedly here, fit into his tragedy as a whole? Later, he will spurn her: does that rejection mark the shallowness and cynicism of his feelings from the start, or should it rather be seen as heartbreaking evidence of a 'noble mind . . . o'erthrown' (III, i, 151)?

Shakespeare's drama derives much of its emotional impact in performance from the unceasing play it makes between the different perspectives of protagonists and audience. We always know (or think we do) that crucial bit more about what is going on in the action as a whole than the character who happens to be speaking at any given time, and whose position may well be being more deeply undermined with every verse. 'Dramatic irony' of this sort doesn't come much starker than it does in the case of *Othello*: just how are we to take the Moor's words of tenderness to Desdemona, conscious as we are that he is destined to be her murderer? Yet our sense that we see further ahead than Othello does is matched by our conviction that we see deeper than he does into his own soul: Shakespeare's characters are not necessarily the most competent judges of either their own or others' motives. Called upon to explain Desdemona's love for him, Othello (I, iii, 127–68) delivers a magnificently misguided account of how, hearing of his military exploits (the grounds, it is apparent, of Othello's own self-esteem), 'She lov'd me for the dangers I had pass'd, / And I loved her that she did pity them.' Desdemona's own explanation, a few lines later (I, iii, 245), gives no hint that she regards herself as an award for valour: '. . . I did love the Moor to live with him,' she says simply.

The wary reader will, therefore, allow for both the circumstances in which a speech is being made and the personality of the speaker who is making it. No passage in Shakespeare can be read purely on its own terms as a generalized and universal statement on love (or, for that matter, on anything else). There are reasons, indeed, for believing that Shakespeare may have had his suspicions of more idealistically abstracted views of love: think how readily Othello's veneration sinks into squalid violence once it comes up against a workaday reality. Believing she has fallen for his heroic story, he finds his wife's living, lusting love for him in person impossible to cope with: if she can feel these things for him, his subconscious clearly reasons, couldn't she feel them for someone else?

No such brutishness of feeling besmirches the exalted sentiments of Sonnet 116, which has often, accordingly, been granted special status as the 'official' Shakespearean pronouncement on what love should be:

Let me not to the marriage of true minds
Admit impediments; love is not love
Which alters when it alteration finds
Or bends with the remover to remove.
O, no, it is an ever-fixèd mark
That looks on tempests and is never shaken;
It is the star to every wandering bark,
Whose worth's unknown, although his height be taken.
Love's not Time's fool, though rosy lips and cheeks
Within his bending sickle's compass come;
Love alters not with his brief hours and weeks,
But bears it out even to the edge of doom.
   If this be error, and upon me proved,
   I never writ, nor no man ever loved.

An inspiring vision of love, there's no doubt, and yet you might say too that it's an inspiring vision of something unattainable, even unreal: the 'star' stays fixed and unalterable only by virtue of its infinite distance. The cynic might even wonder if there isn't a note of desperation in the insistent legalism of the final couplet, and ask whether indeed any man (or woman) ever *did* love in so self-abnegating a fashion. Yet while it doesn't come from a play, this sonnet still has its own context in a larger sonnet-sequence in which the limitations of love, and its attendant agonies, are vividly captured. The shifting moods of the Sonnets as a whole, with their tantalizingly fragmentary dramatization of the developing relationship between poet, 'Youth' and 'Dark Lady', would call such high-flown sentiments into question even if the sonnet didn't raise implicit doubts of its own. The general rule in reading Shakespeare – in so far as there can be any generalization about a body of work so extraordinary in its range – is that nothing should be taken entirely at face value.

'Madam, you have bereft me of all words,' says Bassanio to Portia in *The Merchant of Venice* (III, ii, 175): everyone knows what it is to be struck dumb by deep emotion. No Shakespearean character could ever be truly lost for words for long, though: language is the world they live in and the air that even the least apparently eloquent breathe (think of the dazzling inarticulacy of Henry V in his courtship of Katherine). Rather than sinking into silence, Shakespeare's men and women are far more likely to find themselves carried away by their own rhetoric: the fate, it could be argued, of Othello and the poet-persona of the Sonnets. Both these figures dramatize the profoundly paradoxical sense which Shakespeare has of language: the medium through which the truth is explored and expressed is also that of deceit and self-deception. Trust in the truth of language and we always risk being deceived; reject it and we lose the very possibility of understanding. That most 'poetic' of emotions, love illustrates this paradox to perfection, bringing together the most idealistic selflessness and the most urgently compelling individual desires. In the overwrought rhetoric which characterizes it, love talk all but advertises its artificiality – yet few feelings are experienced so sincerely.

Hence, surely, the centrality of love in Shakespeare's works – a centrality which goes far beyond the supposed demands of dramatic convention for some sort of 'love interest'. Shakespeare did not, it goes without saying, invent love; nor was he the first dramatist to present love on the stage, but he found an altogether new way of appreciating its dramatic force and its symbolic implications. Key to his vision was his perception of love as the quintessentially creative human impulse – the emotion that could, in the eyes of her devoted swain, transform a simple shepherd-girl into an earthly goddess; or, directed inward, turn a cocky and self-centred young blade into a humble supplicant. These transformative powers make love closely analogous with poetry, in which a metaphor may make a woman into a flower, and with the theatre itself, in which the donning of a costume and a set of gestures turns an actor into any character the playwright pleases.

One mundane moral may be drawn from the theatrical experience: that things may not always be as they seem, and indeed our feelings of love may prove in hindsight to have been as unreal as any stage play. (We forget almost as easily as Romeo did himself that the great lover's first flamboyant speeches in praise of love were lavished not on Juliet at all but on another girl entirely, Rosaline!) Yet Shakespeare ventures beyond such worldly scepticism to hint at a far more interesting, profound possibility: that shows and seemings may be the way to a deeper truth.

Nowhere are the revelatory powers of love and theatre more memorably represented than they are in that climactic scene in *A Winter's Tale* in which the statue of Queen Hermione seems to come to life before her long-estranged husband. Astonished at what appears to be a miraculous transformation, King Leontes appreciates for the first time both his wife's true worth and the wrong he has done her over so many years. The cross-dressing of so many Shakespearean heroines setting off to seek their men makes lighter play with these same paradoxes, their disguises becoming the guarantees of their authenticity. The warning that Shakespeare's writings should not be taken too much at face value must therefore be accompanied by another one: that if we aren't prepared to engage openly with them they can do nothing for us at all.

If a poem like Sonnet 116 can't be read 'straight', how susceptible is it to what critics would now call a 'queer' reading? What, if anything, do we know of Shakespeare's own feelings of love? In a more innocent age, scholars fretted about the fact that the great man had made a point of bequeathing his 'second best bed' to his wife Ann Hathaway in his will; today many question whether he was even heterosexual. Inevitably, the discussion has centred upon the Sonnets, with their impassioned addresses to the 'fair youth', and just as inevitably it has been fiercely controversial, with conservative critics determined to save Shakespeare from what they have seen as a shameful stigma upon Britain's Bard, and a more radical group claiming that Shakespeare was quite obviously 'gay'. Sonnet 20 is perhaps the most hotly contested critical territory of all in this regard, the ambiguity of the poet's position being clear from the opening couplet:

A woman's face with Nature's own hand painted,
Hast thou, the master-mistress of my passion . . .

As the sonnet moves towards its conclusion, that ambiguity either finds resolution or deepens, according to one's point of view:

And for a woman wert thou first created,
Till Nature as she wrought thee fell a-doting,
And by addition me of thee defeated
By adding one thing to my purpose nothing.
  But since she pricked thee out for women's pleasure,
  Mine be thy love, and thy love's use their treasure.

That nature is said to have 'defeated' the poet when she 'pricked' the young man out with a penis has often been taken as triumphant vindication by those who have taken on the task of protecting Shakespeare from any suggestion of deviancy, yet as a heterosexualist manifesto it leaves a certain amount to be desired. Scholars suggest that the word 'use' in the final line may refer to the fact of reproduction rather than (as has often been assumed) the act of sex, leaving the question of whether sexual contact took place between poet and young man still unresolved. And, leaving that most mechanistic of questions aside, what does the sonnet say of the poet's broader sensibility? What heterosexual man would even think of addressing another in such terms as these, however 'platonic' the relationship implied?

The further we get into these questions, the more confusing it all becomes: what, in the end, do we know of hetero- or homosexuality at a stage in history almost three centuries before either of these things had been fully conceptualized? The idea that one might have a deep-centred sexual 'orientation', which would in turn underpin an overall 'identity', has been a much more recent development than might immediately be assumed. How the passions were ordered and articulated before that remains uncertain. As far as specific sexual practices were concerned, of course, there is comparatively little that modernity could have taught Merrie England: if anything, Shakespeare's countrymen may have been more indulgent towards homosexual acts. While heterosexual marriage was clearly the flagship state, it has been suggested that a blind eye may fairly readily have been turned towards discreet departures from this respectable norm, whether with wenches or boys. That said, since this easy-going attitude seems to have extended to a far more affectionate and physically demonstrative manner between males in general, there may be rather less to an apparent intimacy than meets the eye. So, do these different cultural conditions safely explain away Shakespeare's attachment to his Youth, or do they make a sexual relationship seem more likely? If the latter possibility appeals, we have to consider why a homosexual Shakespeare would spend the first seventeen sonnets of his sequence exhorting his young lover to marry and reproduce. There are other puzzles too, of course, not least that of what we are to make of the mysterious 'Dark Lady', with whom the poet of the Sonnets has – however ungratefully – been sleeping.

The high-minded answer to all these questions is that the sonnets are only poems, projections of the imagination, the Youth, the Dark Lady – and even the speaking 'poet' – no more real than any of the characters of Shakespeare's plays. We should enjoy these poems *as* poems, appreciate the drama implicit in them on its own terms: to seek any deeper is to descend into the realms of gossip. Few readers have the iron critical will required to maintain that sort of detachment with complete conviction, yet, however human the desire to fathom the whole thing out, the fact remains that any final, definitive answer is going to elude us. We may well have our hunches about the nature of Shakespeare's sexuality, but the data simply don't exist that would enable us to state with confidence that Shakespeare either was or wasn't homosexual in any modern sense. That question has to join the lengthy list of other things we don't know about the most celebrated writer in the English language – including such small matters as his religious beliefs and politics.

A Note on the Text

There is no single, definitive edition of the works of Shakespeare. The texts we use today are largely based on those of the First Folio edition put together in 1623 by John Heminges and Henry Condell. As former colleagues of the author in the theatre, they were in as good a position as anyone to know what he had written, but the Bard himself had been dead seven years by the time their edition appeared, and it did not carry his imprimatur. Editors have, as a result, felt licensed to add preferred readings from other early texts. Often enough these 'Quartos' were cobbled together from memory and published opportunistically as pirate editions: in some cases, though, they have contained enduring poetry.

'Shakespeare' is a fluid concept, then, but to make matters more difficult still, he is known to have collaborated at one time or another with a number of different writers. It follows that not everything in the plays can be automatically assumed to be his, and there have been unseemly scholarly tugs of war over certain passages. These include, as it happens, some of those given here from *Henry VI Part 1* as well as those from *The Two Noble Kinsmen*. It is more than likely that the speeches of the jailer's daughter in that play were written by Shakespeare's collaborator John Fletcher: they are included here because they are good poetry, and a part of that canon of work we have come to know as 'Shakespeare'. Modern editions of Shakespeare have had the benefit of recent advances in textual scholarship – and the disadvantage of having been prepared four centuries after they were originally written. There is no such thing as certainty, then, where Shakespeare is concerned. Editors and readers may always differ over interpretations – even actual wordings: that is part of the fun of reading Shakespeare.

The text used in this book is in most cases taken from the New Penguin Shakespeare editions of the plays and the line references given correspond to these.

Two Gentlemen of Verona

[II, iv, 126–39] *Valentine, once scathing about Love and the absurdities it drove men to, must admit to his friend Proteus that he too has now been humbled:*

I have done penance for contemning Love,
Whose high imperious thoughts have punished me
With bitter fasts, with penitential groans,
With nightly tears and daily heart-sore sighs;
For, in revenge of my contempt of Love,
Love hath chased sleep from my enthralled eyes
And made them watchers of mine own heart's sorrow.
O gentle Proteus, Love's a mighty lord,
And hath so humbled me as I confess
There is no woe to his correction,
Nor to his service no such joy on earth.
Now no discourse, except it be of Love;
Now can I break my fast, dine, sup, and sleep,
Upon the very naked name of Love.

[II, vii, 15–38] *Her servant Lucetta having sought to dissuade her from following Proteus on his travels, Julia condemns her for her heartlessness and lack of understanding:*

O, know'st thou not his looks are my soul's food?
Pity the dearth that I have pined in
By longing for that food so long a time.
Didst thou but know the inly touch of love,
Thou wouldst as soon go kindle fire with snow
As seek to quench the fire of love with words.

LUCETTA
I do not seek to quench your love's hot fire,
But qualify the fire's extreme rage,
Lest it should burn above the bounds of reason.

JULIA
The more thou dam'st it up, the more it burns.
The current that with gentle murmur glides,
Thou know'st, being stopp'd, impatiently doth rage;
But when his fair course is not hindered,
He makes sweet music with th' enamell'd stones,
Giving a gentle kiss to every sedge
He overtaketh in his pilgrimage.
And so by many winding nooks he strays
With willing sport to the wild ocean.
Then let me go, and hinder not my course.
I'll be as patient as a gentle stream
And make a pastime of each weary step,
Till the last step have brought me to my love;
And there I'll rest as, after much turmoil,
A blessed soul doth in Elysium.

Valentine, now apparently an expert in the arts of love, is consulted by his beloved Silvia's father, the aged Duke. Jewels, Valentine suggests, may be a girl's best friend, but cunningly contrived flattery comes a close second:

DUKE

There is a lady in Verona here
Whom I affect, but she is nice and coy
And nought esteems my aged eloquence.
Now, therefore would I have thee to my tutor –
For long agone I have forgot to court;
Besides, the fashion of the time is changed –
How and which way I may bestow myself
To be regarded in her sun-bright eye.

VALENTINE

Win her with gifts, if she respect not words.
Dumb jewels often in their silent kind
More than quick words do move a woman's mind.

DUKE

But she did scorn a present that I sent her.

VALENTINE

A woman sometime scorns what best contents her.
Send her another; never give her o'er,
For scorn at first makes after-love the more.
If she do frown, 'tis not in hate of you,
But rather to beget more love in you.
If she do chide, 'tis not to have you gone,
For why the fools are mad if left alone.
Take no repulse, whatever she doth say;
For 'get you gone', she doth not mean 'away'.
Flatter and praise, commend, extol their graces;

Though ne'er so black, say they have angels' faces.
That man that hath a tongue, I say, is no man,
If with his tongue he cannot win a woman.

[III, ii, 67–86] *Asked for assistance by Valentine's foolish rival Thurio, Proteus tells him he will have to do some of the work himself – poetry, he says, is the way to catch a lady:*

But you, Sir Thurio, are not sharp enough.
You must lay lime to tangle her desires
By wailful sonnets, whose composed rhymes
Should be full-fraught with serviceable vows . . .
Say that upon the altar of her beauty
You sacrifice your tears, your sighs, your heart.
Write till your ink be dry, and with your tears
Moist it again, and frame some feeling line
That may discover such integrity;
For Orpheus' lute was strung with poets' sinews,
Whose golden touch could soften steel and stones,
Make tigers tame, and huge leviathans
Forsake unsounded deeps to dance on sands.
After your dire-lamenting elegies,
Visit by night your lady's chamber window
With some sweet consort. To their instruments
Tune a deploring dump; the night's dead silence
Will well become such sweet-complaining grievance.
This, or else nothing, will inherit her.

Henry VI Part 2

[III, ii, 333–66] *Ordered into exile by an angry King, Suffolk regrets only his separation from the Queen, his secret lover:*

         . . . Will you bid me leave?
Now, by the ground that I am banished from,
Well could I curse away a winter's night,
Though standing naked on a mountain top
Where biting cold would never let grass grow,
And think it but a minute spent in sport.
QUEEN
O, let me entreat thee cease. Give me thy hand,
That I may dew it with my mournful tears;
Nor let the rain of heaven wet this place
To wash away my woeful monuments.
O, could this kiss be printed in thy hand,
That thou mightst think upon these by the seal,
Through whom a thousand sighs are breathed for thee.
So get thee gone, that I may know my grief.
'Tis but surmised whiles thou art standing by,
As one that surfeits, thinking on a want.
I will repeal thee, or, be well assured,
Adventure to be banishèd myself;
And banishèd I am, if but from thee.
Go, speak not to me. Even now be gone.
O, go not yet. Even thus two friends condemned

Embrace and kiss and take ten thousand leaves,
Loather a hundred times to part than die.
Yet now farewell, and farewell life with thee.

SUFFOLK
Thus is poor Suffolk ten times banishèd,
Once by the King and three times thrice by thee.
'Tis not the land I care for, wert thou thence.
A wilderness is populous enough,
So Suffolk had thy heavenly company;
For where thou art, there is the world itself
With every several pleasure in the world;
And where thou art not, desolation.
I can no more. Live thou to joy thy life;
Myself no joy in nought, but that thou livest.

Titus Andronicus

[II, i, 1–24] *Aaron, the machiavellian Moor, sees his lover's marriage to the emperor as his own path to power:*

Now climbeth Tamora Olympus' top,
Safe out of fortune's shot, and sits aloft,
Secure of thunder's crack or lightning flash,
Advanced above pale envy's threat'ning reach.
As when the golden sun salutes the morn
And, having gilt the ocean with his beams,
Gallops the zodiac in his glistering coach
And overlooks the highest-peering hills,
So Tamora.
Upon her wit doth earthly honour wait,
And virtue stoops and trembles at her frown.
Then, Aaron, arm thy heart and fit thy thoughts
To mount aloft with thy imperial mistress,
And mount her pitch, whom thou in triumph long
Hast prisoner held, fettered in amorous chains,
And faster bound to Aaron's charming eyes
Than is Prometheus tied to Caucasus.
Away with slavish weeds and servile thoughts!
I will be bright and shine in pearl and gold
To wait upon this new-made Empress.
'To wait' said I? – to wanton with this queen,
This goddess, this Semiramis, this nymph,

This siren that will charm Rome's Saturnine,
And see his shipwreck and his commonweal's.

[II, i, 79–87] *Aaron may be calculating, but his friend
Demetrius is more cynical still:*

CHIRON
Aaron, a thousand deaths
Would I propose to achieve her whom I love.
AARON
To achieve her – how?
DEMETRIUS
Why makes thou it so strange?
She is a woman, therefore may be wooed;
She is a woman, therefore may be won;
She is Lavinia, therefore must be loved.
What, man, more water glideth by the mill
Than wots the miller of, and easy it is
Of a cut loaf to steal a shive, we know.

Henry VI Part 1

[V, v, 55–65] *The Duke of Suffolk takes a romantically disapproving view of the royal tradition of arranged marriage (though, ironically, he is actually furthering his own amorous ends):*

Marriage is a matter of more worth
Than to be dealt in by attorneyship;
Not whom we will, but whom his grace affects,
Must be companion of his nuptial bed.
And therefore, lords, since he affects her most,
It most of all these reasons bindeth us
In our opinions she should be preferred.
For what is wedlock forcèd but a hell,
An age of discord and continual strife?
Whereas the contrary bringeth bliss
And is a pattern of celestial peace.

Richard III

[I, ii, 227–63] *Unprepossessing, unlikeable and generally unaccustomed to inspiring affection of any kind, Richard Crookback is captivated by the sexual hold he senses he has over Lady Anne – a woman with every imaginable reason to hate him:*

Was ever woman in this humour wooed?
Was ever woman in this humour won?
I'll have her, but I will not keep her long.
What! I that killed her husband and his father
To take her in her heart's extremest hate,
With curses in her mouth, tears in her eyes,
The bleeding witness of my hatred by,
Having God, her conscience, and these bars against me,
And I no friends to back my suit at all
But the plain devil and dissembling looks?
And yet to win her! All the world to nothing!
Ha!
Hath she forgot already that brave prince,
Edward, her lord, whom I, some three months since,
Stabbed in my angry mood at Tewkesbury?
A sweeter and a lovelier gentleman,
Framed in the prodigality of nature,
Young, valiant, wise, and, no doubt, right royal,
The spacious world cannot again afford;

And will she yet abase her eyes on me,
That cropped the golden prime of this sweet prince
And made her widow to a woeful bed?
On me, whose all not equals Edward's moiety?
On me, that halts and am misshapen thus?
My dukedom to a beggarly denier
I do mistake my person all this while!
Upon my life, she finds, although I cannot,
Myself to be a marvellous proper man.
I'll be at charges for a looking-glass
And entertain a score or two of tailors
To study fashions to adorn my body;
Since I am crept in favour with myself
I will maintain it with some little cost.
But first I'll turn yon fellow in his grave,
And then return lamenting to my love.
Shine out, fair sun, till I have bought a glass,
That I may see my shadow as I pass.

Comedy of Errors

[II, ii, 119–55] *For Adriana, her husband Antipholus'*
(apparent) infidelity and indifference represent a violent
separation within her own self:

Ay, ay, Antipholus, look strange and frown.
Some other mistress hath thy sweet aspects.
I am not Adriana, nor thy wife.
The time was once when thou unurged wouldst vow
That never words were music to thine ear,
That never object pleasing in thine eye,
That never touch well welcome to thy hand,
That never meat sweet-savoured in thy taste,
Unless I spake, or looked, or touched, or carved to thee.
How comes it now, my husband, O how comes it,
That thou art then estrangèd from thyself?
Thyself I call it, being strange to me
That, undividable, incorporate,
Am better than thy dear self's better part.
Ah, do not tear away thyself from me;
For know, my love, as easy mayst thou fall
A drop of water in the breaking gulf,
And take unmingled thence that drop again
Without addition or diminishing,
As take from me thyself, and not me too.
How dearly would it touch thee to the quick

Shouldst thou but hear I were licentious,
And that this body consecrate to thee
By ruffian lust should be contaminate?
Wouldst thou not spit at me, and spurn at me,
And hurl the name of husband in my face,
And tear the stained skin off my harlot brow,
And from my false hand cut the wedding ring,
And break it with a deep-divorcing vow?
I know thou canst, and therefore see thou do it.
I am possessed with an adulterate blot.
My blood is mingled with the crime of lust;
For if we two be one, and thou play false,
I do digest the poison of thy flesh,
Being strumpeted by thy contagion.
Keep then fair league and truce with thy true bed,
I live unstained, thou undishonourèd.

Love's Labour's Lost

[III, i, 170–202] *Berowne – who has always prided himself on his sophistication and cynicism – is aghast at his own subjection to Dan (Lord) Cupid:*

And I, forsooth, in love!
I, that have been love's whip,
A very beadle to a humorous sigh,
A critic, nay, a night-watch constable,
A domineering pedant o'er the boy,
Than whom no mortal so magnificent!
This wimpled, whining, purblind, wayward boy,
This Signor Junior, giant-dwarf, Dan Cupid,
Regent of love-rhymes, lord of folded arms,
Th'anointed sovereign of sighs and groans,
Liege of all loiterers and malcontents,
Dread prince of plackets, king of codpieces,
Sole imperator and great general
Of trotting paritors – O my little heart!
And I to be a corporal of his field,
And wear his colours like a tumbler's hoop!
What? I love? I sue? I seek a wife?
A woman, that is like a German clock,
Still a-repairing, ever out of frame,
And never going aright, being a watch,
But being watched that it may still go right!

Nay, to be perjured, which is worst of all;
And among three to love the worst of all –
A whitely wanton with a velvet brow,
With two pitch-balls stuck in her face for eyes;
Ay, and, by heaven, one that will do the deed
Though Argus were her eunuch and her guard!
And I to sigh for her, to watch for her,
To pray for her! Go to, it is a plague
That Cupid will impose for my neglect
Of his almighty dreadful little might.
Well, I will love, write, sigh, pray, sue, and groan;
Some men must love my lady, and some Joan.

[IV, iii, 294–344] *He and his friends all having abjectly failed*
in their vows to shun womankind in favour of seclusion and
study, Berowne at least has his wits about him sufficiently to
rationalize the situation:

O, we have made a vow to study, lords,
And in that vow we have forsworn our books;
For when would you, my liege, or you, or you,
In leaden contemplation have found out
Such fiery numbers as the prompting eyes
Of beauty's tutors have enriched you with?
Other slow arts entirely keep the brain,
And therefore, finding barren practisers,
Scarce show a harvest of their heavy toil;
But love, first learnèd in a lady's eyes,
Lives not alone immurèd in the brain,
But with the motion of all elements

Courses as swift as thought in every power,
And gives to every power a double power,
Above their functions and their offices.
It adds a precious seeing to the eye:
A lover's eyes will gaze an eagle blind.
A lover's ear will hear the lowest sound
When the suspicious head of theft is stopped.
Love's feeling is more soft and sensible
Than are the tender horns of cockled snails.
Love's tongue proves dainty Bacchus gross in taste.
For valour, is not Love a Hercules,
Still climbing trees in the Hesperides?
Subtle as Sphinx; as sweet and musical
As bright Apollo's lute, strung with his hair.
And when Love speaks, the voice of all the gods
Make heaven drowsy with the harmony.
Never durst poet touch a pen to write
Until his ink were tempered with Love's sighs.
O, then his lines would ravish savage ears
And plant in tyrants mild humility.
From women's eyes this doctrine I derive:
They sparkle still the right Promethean fire;
They are the books, the arts, the academes,
That show, contain, and nourish all the world;
Else none at all in aught proves excellent.
Then fools you were these women to forswear,
Or, keeping what is sworn, you will prove fools.
For wisdom's sake, a word that all men love,
Or for love's sake, a word that loves all men,
Or for men's sake, the authors of these women,
Or women's sake, by whom we men are men –

Let us once lose our oaths to find ourselves,
Or else we lose ourselves to keep our oaths.
It is religion to be thus forsworn,
For charity itself fulfils the law,
And who can sever love from charity?

KING
Saint Cupid, then! And, soldiers, to the field!

BEROWNE
Advance your standards, and upon them, lords!
Pell-mell, down with them!

A Midsummer Night's Dream

[I, i, 28–38] *Egeus, angry father of Hermia, sees Lysander's love for her as a calculated theft of her sense of daughterly duty:*

Thou, thou, Lysander, thou hast given her rhymes,
And interchanged love-tokens with my child.
Thou hast by moonlight at her window sung
With feigning voice verses of feigning love,
And stolen the impression of her fantasy.
With bracelets of thy hair, rings, gauds, conceits,
Knacks, trifles, nosegays, sweetmeats – messengers
Of strong prevailment in unhardened youth –
With cunning hast thou filched my daughter's heart,
Turned her obedience which is due to me
To stubborn harshness.

[I, i, 128–55] *Lysander and Hermia discourse in duet on the crosses customarily encountered by love – and on the need for romance to be tempered with steely stoicism:*

LYSANDER
How now, my love? Why is your cheek so pale?
How chance the roses there do fade so fast?
HERMIA
Belike for want of rain, which I could well

Beteem them from the tempest of my eyes.

LYSANDER

Ay me! for aught that I could ever read,
Could ever hear by tale or history,
The course of true love never did run smooth;
But either it was different in blood –

HERMIA

O cross! – too high to be enthralled to low.

LYSANDER

Or else misgraffèd in respect of years–

HERMIA

O spite! – too old to be engaged to young.

LYSANDER

Or else it stood upon the choice of friends –

HERMIA

O hell! – to choose love by another's eyes.

LYSANDER

Or if there were a sympathy in choice,
War, death, or sickness did lay siege to it,
Making it momentany as a sound,
Swift as a shadow, short as any dream,
Brief as the lightning in the collied night,
That in a spleen unfolds both heaven and earth,
And – ere a man hath power to say 'Behold!' –
The jaws of darkness do devour it up.
So quick bright things come to confusion.

HERMIA

If then true lovers have been ever crossed
It stands as an edict in destiny.
Then let us teach our trial patience,
Because it is a customary cross,

As due to love as thoughts, and dreams, and sighs,
Wishes, and tears – poor fancy's followers.

[I, i, 226–45] *Helena ponders the injustice of love, and its
apparent obliviousness to all objective standards:*

How happy some o'er other some can be!
Through Athens I am thought as fair as she.
But what of that? Demetrius thinks not so;
He will not know what all but he do know.
And as he errs, doting on Hermia's eyes,
So I, admiring of his qualities.
Things base and vile, holding no quantity,
Love can transpose to form and dignity,
Love looks not with the eyes, but with the mind,
And therefore is winged Cupid painted blind.
Nor hath love's mind of any judgment taste;
Wings and no eyes figure unheedy haste.
And therefore is love said to be a child
Because in choice he is so oft beguiled.
As waggish boys in game themselves forswear,
So the boy love is perjured everywhere;
For ere Demetrius looked on Hermia's eyne
He hailed down oaths that he was only mine,
And when this hail some heat from Hermia felt,
So he dissolved, and showers of oaths did melt.

Romeo and Juliet

[I, iii, 80–95] *Lady Capulet asks her daughter, Juliet, to consider the qualities of Paris, the man she would like to see her take as her husband:*

What say you? Can you love the gentleman?
This night you shall behold him at our feast.
Read o'er the volume of young Paris' face,
And find delight writ there with beauty's pen.
Examine every married lineament,
And see how one another lends content.
And what obscured in this fair volume lies
Find written in the margent of his eyes.
This precious book of love, this unbound lover,
To beautify him only lacks a cover.
The fish lives in the sea, and 'tis much pride
For fair without the fair within to hide.
That book in many's eyes doth share the glory,
That in gold clasps locks in the golden story.
So shall you share all that he doth possess,
By having him making yourself no less.

[I, v, 44–53] Love at first sight, when Romeo sets eyes on Juliet, after stealing incognito into the Capulet family's ball:

O, she doth teach the torches to burn bright!
It seems she hangs upon the cheek of night
Like a rich jewel in an Ethiop's ear –
Beauty too rich for use, for earth too dear!
So shows a snowy dove trooping with crows
As yonder lady o'er her fellows shows.
The measure done, I'll watch her place of stand
And, touching hers, make blessèd my rude hand.
Did my heart love till now? Forswear it, sight!
For I ne'er saw true beauty till this night.

[II, ii, 2–185] Romeo is below Juliet's window, in Lord Capulet's orchard, as the famous 'balcony scene' begins – a dangerous place for any member of the hated Montague clan to be found lurking:

But soft! What light through yonder window breaks?
It is the East, and Juliet is the sun!
Arise, fair sun, and kill the envious moon,
Who is already sick and pale with grief
That thou her maid art far more fair than she.
Be not her maid, since she is envious.
Her vestal livery is but sick and green,
And none but fools do wear it. Cast it off.
It is my lady. O, it is my love!
O that she knew she were!
She speaks. Yet she says nothing. What of that?

Her eye discourses. I will answer it.
I am too bold. 'Tis not to me she speaks.
Two of the fairest stars in all the heaven,
Having some business, do entreat her eyes
To twinkle in their spheres till they return.
What if her eyes were there, they in her head?
The brightness of her cheek would shame those stars
As daylight doth a lamp. Her eyes in heaven
Would through the airy region stream so bright
That birds would sing and think it were not night.
See how she leans her cheek upon her hand!
O that I were a glove upon that hand,
That I might touch that cheek!

JULIET

       Ay me!

ROMEO

          She speaks.
O, speak again, bright angel! – for thou art
As glorious to this night, being o'er my head,
As is a wingèd messenger of heaven
Unto the white-upturnèd wondering eyes
Of mortals that fall back to gaze on him
When he bestrides the lazy, puffing clouds
And sails upon the bosom of the air.

JULIET

O Romeo, Romeo! – wherefore art thou Romeo?
Deny thy father and refuse thy name!
Or, if thou wilt not, be but sworn my love,
And I'll no longer be a Capulet.

ROMEO (*aside*)

Shall I hear more, or shall I speak at this?

JULIET

'Tis but thy name that is my enemy.
Thou art thyself, though not a Montague.
What's Montague? It is nor hand, nor foot
Nor arm nor face nor any other part
Belonging to a man. O, be some other name!
What's in a name? That which we call a rose
By any other name would smell as sweet.
So Romeo would, were he not Romeo called,
Retain that dear perfection which he owes
Without that title. Romeo, doff thy name;
And for that name, which is no part of thee,
Take all myself.

ROMEO

              I take thee at thy word.
Call me but love, and I'll be new baptized.
Henceforth I never will be Romeo.

JULIET

What man art thou that, thus bescreened in night,
So stumblest on my counsel?

ROMEO

                  By a name
I know not how to tell thee who I am.
My name, dear saint, is hateful to myself,
Because it is an enemy to thee.
Had I it written, I would tear the word.

JULIET

My ears have yet not drunk a hundred words
Of thy tongue's uttering, yet I know the sound.
Art thou not Romeo, and a Montague?

ROMEO
Neither, fair maid, if either thee dislike.

JULIET
How camest thou hither, tell me, and wherefore?
The orchard walls are high and hard to climb,
And the place death, considering who thou art,
If any of my kinsmen find thee here.

ROMEO
With love's light wings did I o'erperch these walls;
For stony limits cannot hold love out,
And what love can do, that dares love attempt.
Therefore thy kinsmen are no stop to me.

JULIET
If they do see thee, they will murther thee.

ROMEO
Alack, there lies more peril in thine eye
Than twenty of their swords! Look thou but sweet,
And I am proof against their enmity.

JULIET
I would not for the world they saw thee here.

ROMEO
I have night's cloak to hide me from their eyes;
And but thou love me, let them find me here.
My life were better ended by their hate
Than death proroguèd, wanting of thy love.

JULIET
By whose direction foundest thou out this place?

ROMEO
By love, that first did prompt me to inquire.
He lent me counsel, and I lent him eyes.

I am no pilot; yet, wert thou as far
As that vast shore washed with the farthest sea,
I would adventure for such merchandise.

JULIET

Thou knowest the mask of night is on my face,
Else would a maiden blush bepaint my cheek
For that which thou hast heard me speak tonight.
Fain would I dwell on form – fain, fain deny
What I have spoke. But farewell compliment!
Dost thou love me, I know thou wilt say 'Ay'.
And I will take thy word. Yet, if thou swearest,
Thou mayst prove false. At lovers' perjuries,
They say, Jove laughs. O gentle Romeo,
If thou dost love, pronounce it faithfully.
Or if thou thinkest I am too quickly won,
I'll frown, and be perverse, and say thee nay,
So thou wilt woo. But else, not for the world.
In truth, fair Montague, I am too fond,
And therefore thou mayst think my 'haviour light.
But trust me, gentleman, I'll prove more true
Than those that have more cunning to be strange.
I should have been more strange, I must confess,
But that thou overheardest, ere I was ware,
My true-love passion. Therefore pardon me,
And not impute this yielding to light love,
Which the dark night hath so discoverèd.

ROMEO

Lady, by yonder blessèd moon I vow,
That tips with silver all these fruit-tree tops –

JULIET

O, swear not by the moon, th' inconstant moon,

That monthly changes in her circled orb,
Lest that thy love prove likewise variable.

ROMEO

What shall I swear by?

JULIET

Do not swear at all.
Or if thou wilt, swear by thy gracious self,
Which is the god of my idolatry,
And I'll believe thee.

ROMEO

If my heart's dear love –

JULIET

Well, do not swear. Although I joy in thee,
I have no joy of this contract tonight.
It is too rash, too unadvised, too sudden;
Too like the lightning, which doth cease to be
Ere one can say 'It lightens.' Sweet, good night!
This bud of love, by summer's ripening breath,
May prove a beauteous flower when next we meet.
Good night, good night! As sweet repose and rest
Come to thy heart as that within my breast!

ROMEO

O, wilt thou leave me so unsatisfied?

JULIET

What satisfaction canst thou have tonight?

ROMEO

Th' exchange of thy love's faithful vow for mine.

JULIET

I gave thee mine before thou didst request it.
And yet I would it were to give again.

ROMEO

Wouldst thou withdraw it? For what purpose, love?

JULIET

But to be frank and give it thee again.
And yet I wish but for the thing I have.
My bounty is as boundless as the sea,
My love as deep. The more I give to thee,
The more I have, for both are infinite.
I hear some noise within. Dear love, adieu! . . .

Enter Juliet above, again

JULIET

Hist! Romeo, hist! O for a falconer's voice,
To lure this tassel-gentle back again!
Bondage is hoarse and may not speak aloud,
Else would I tear the cave where Echo lies
And make her airy tongue more hoarse than mine
With repetition of 'My Romeo!'
. . . 'Tis almost morning. I would have thee gone –
And yet no farther than a wanton's bird,
That lets it hop a little from his hand,
Like a poor prisoner in his twisted gyves,
And with a silk thread plucks it back again,
So loving-jealous of his liberty.

ROMEO

I would I were thy bird.

JULIET

Sweet, so would I.
Yet I should kill thee with much cherishing.
Good night, good night! Parting is such sweet sorrow,
That I shall say good night till it be morrow.

[II, vi, 9–20] *A voice of age and sobriety, Friar Laurence is filled with foreboding as well as with wonder:*

These violent delights have violent ends
And in their triumph die, like fire and powder,
Which as they kiss consume. The sweetest honey
Is loathsome in his own deliciousness
And in the taste confounds the appetite.
Therefore love moderately. Long love doth so.
Too swift arrives as tardy as too slow.
    Enter Juliet somewhat fast. She embraces Romeo
Here comes the lady. O, so light a foot
Will ne'er wear out the everlasting flint.
A lover may bestride the gossamers
That idles in the wanton summer air,
And yet not fall. So light is vanity.

[III, ii, 1–31] *Juliet, impatient again, longs for sundown, and her rendezvous with Romeo:*

Gallop apace, you fiery-footed steeds,
Towards Phoebus' lodging! Such a waggoner
As Phaëton would whip you to the West
And bring in cloudy night immediately.
Spread thy close curtain, love-performing night,
That runaway's eyes may wink, and Romeo
Leap to these arms untalked of and unseen.
Lovers can see to do their amorous rites
By their own beauties; or, if love be blind,
It best agrees with night. Come, civil night,

Thou sober-suited matron, all in black,
And learn me how to lose a winning match,
Played for a pair of stainless maidenhoods.
Hood my unmanned blood, bating in my cheeks,
With thy black mantle till strange love grow bold,
Think true love acted simple modesty.
Come, night. Come, Romeo. Come, thou day in night;
For thou wilt lie upon the wings of night
Whiter than new snow upon a raven's back.
Come, gentle night. Come, loving, black-browed night.
Give me my Romeo. And when I shall die,
Take him and cut him out in little stars,
And he will make the face of heaven so fine
That all the world will be in love with night
And pay no worship to the garish sun.
O I have bought the mansion of a love,
But not possessed it; and though I am sold,
Not yet enjoyed. So tedious is this day
As is the night before some festival
To an impatient child that hath new robes
And may not wear them.

[III, v, 1–36] *Next morning, her lover should be leaving, and*
now Juliet wants to hold back the passage of time:

JULIET
Wilt thou be gone? It is not yet near day.
It was the nightingale, and not the lark,
That pierced the fearful hollow of thine ear.
Nightly she sings on yond pomegranate tree.

Believe me, love, it was the nightingale.

ROMEO

It was the lark, the herald of the morn;
No nightingale. Look, love, what envious streaks
Do lace the severing clouds in yonder East.
Night's candles are burnt out, and jocund day
Stands tiptoe on the misty mountain tops.
I must be gone and live, or stay and die.

JULIET

Yond light is not daylight; I know it, I.
It is some meteor that the sun exhales
To be to thee this night a torchbearer
And light thee on thy way to Mantua.
Therefore stay yet. Thou needest not to be gone.

ROMEO

Let me be ta'en, let me be put to death.
I am content, so thou wilt have it so.
I'll say yon grey is not the morning's eye;
'Tis but the pale reflex of Cynthia's brow.
Nor that is not the lark whose notes do beat
The vaulty heaven so high above our heads.
I have more care to stay than will to go.
Come, death, and welcome! Juliet wills it so.
How is't, my soul? Let's talk. It is not day.

JULIET

It is, it is! Hie hence, be gone, away!
It is the lark that sings so out of tune,
Straining harsh discords and unpleasing sharps.
Some say the lark makes sweet division.
This doth not so, for she divideth us.
Some say the lark and loathèd toad changed eyes.

O, now I would they had changed voices too,
Since arm from arm that voice doth us affray,
Hunting thee hence with hunt's-up to the day!
O, now be gone! More light and light it grows.

ROMEO

More light and light: more dark and dark our woes!

The Merchant of Venice

[III, ii, 1–24] *In accordance with the will of her late father,*
Portia's portrait is to be found in one of three caskets – gold,
silver and lead. Whichever suitor chooses correctly will have
her hand in marriage. As Bassanio prepares to face the
challenge, Portia finds herself almost babbling – she cannot
bear, she realizes, the thought that he might choose wrongly:

I pray you tarry, pause a day or two
Before you hazard, for, in choosing wrong
I lose your company. Therefore forbear a while.
There's something tells me, but it is not love,
I would not lose you; and you know yourself
Hate counsels not in such a quality.
But lest you should not understand me well –
And yet a maiden hath no tongue but thought –
I would detain you here some month or two
Before you venture for me. I could teach you
How to choose right, but then I am forsworn.
So will I never be. So may you miss me.
But if you do, you'll make me wish a sin,
That I had been forsworn. Beshrew your eyes!
They have o'erlooked me and divided me;
One half of me is yours, the other half yours,
Mine own I would say; but if mine, then yours,
And so all yours. O these naughty times

Puts bars between the owners and their rights.
And so, though yours, not yours. Prove it so,
Let fortune go to hell for it, not I.
I speak too long, but 'tis to peice the time,
To eke it and to draw it out in length,
To stay you from election.

[V, i, 1–24] *On a moonlit night, Lorenzo and Jessica recall some troubled lovers of the mythical past:*

LORENZO
The moon shines bright. In such a night as this,
When the sweet wind did gently kiss the trees
And they did make no noise, in such a night
Troilus methinks mounted the Troyan walls,
And sighed his soul toward the Grecian tents
Where Cressid lay that night.

JESSICA
In such a night
Did Thisbe fearfully o'ertrip the dew,
And saw the lion's shadow ere himself,
And ran dismayed away.

LORENZO
In such a night
Stood Dido with a willow in her hand
Upon the wild sea-banks, and waft her love
To come again to Carthage.

JESSICA
In such a night
Medea gathered the enchanted herbs

That did renew old Aeson.

LORENZO
In such a night
Did Jessica steal from the wealthy Jew,
And with an unthrift love did run from Venice
As far as Belmont.

JESSICA
In such a night
Did young Lorenzo swear he loved her well,
Stealing her soul with many vows of faith,
And ne'er a true one.

LORENZO
In such a night
Did pretty Jessica, like a little shrew,
Slander her love, and he forgave it her.

JESSICA
I would out-night you, did nobody come;
But, hark, I hear the footing of a man.

The Merry Wives of Windsor

[I, iii, 35–77] *The gross and ageing Sir John Falstaff absurdly fancies his chances with not one but two of Windsor's wealthier wives:*

FALSTAFF

My honest lads, I will tell you what I am about.

PISTOL

Two yards, and more.

FALSTAFF

No quips now, Pistol. Indeed, I am in the waist two yards about. But I am now about no waste – I am about thrift. Briefly, I do mean to make love to Ford's wife. I spy entertainment in her; she discourses, she carves, she gives the leer of invitation. I can construe the action of her familiar style; and the hardest voice of her behaviour – to be Englished rightly – is 'I am Sir John Falstaff's.'

PISTOL

He hath studied her well, and translated her will out of honesty into English.

NYM

The anchor is deep. Will that humour pass?

FALSTAFF

Now, the report goes she has all the rule of her husband's purse. He hath a legion of angels.

PISTOL
As many devils entertain! And 'To her, boy,' say I.

NYM
The humour rises – it is good. Humour me the angels.

FALSTAFF
I have writ me here a letter to her; and here
another to Page's wife, who even now gave me good
eyes too, examined my parts with most judicious
oeillades. Sometimes the beam of her view gilded
my foot, sometimes my portly belly.

PISTOL
Then did the sun on dunghill shine.

NYM
I thank thee for that humour.

FALSTAFF
O, she did so course o'er my exteriors with such a greedy
intention that the appetite of her eye did seem to scorch
me up like a burning-glass. Here's another letter to her.
She bears the purse too. She is a region in Guiana, all
gold and bounty. I will be cheaters to them both, and
they shall be exchequers to me. They shall be my East
and West Indies, and I will trade to them both. Go, bear
thou this letter to Mistress Page; (to Nym) and thou this
to Mistress Ford. We will thrive, lads, we will thrive.

PISTOL
Shall I Sir Pandarus of Troy become –
And by my side wear steel? Then Lucifer take all!

NYM
I will run no base humour. Here, take the humour-letter.
I will keep the haviour of reputation.

FALSTAFF [to Robin]

Hold, sirrah, bear you these letters tightly;
Sail like my pinnace to these golden shores.
Rogues, hence, avaunt! Vanish like hailstones, go!
Trudge, plod away o' th' hoof, seek shelter, pack!
Falstaff will learn the humour of the age,
French thrift, you rogues – myself, and skirted page.

[II, i, 1–29] *But one recipient, Mrs Page, is not best pleased:*

What! have I 'scaped love letters in the holiday time of
my beauty, and am I now a subject for them? Let me see.
She reads
Ask me no reason why I love you, for though Love use Reason
for his precisian, he admits him not for his counsellor. You are
not young, no more am I. Go to, then, there's sympathy. You
are merry, so am I. Ha! ha! then there's more sympathy. You
love sack, and so do I. Would you desire better sympathy? Let
it suffice thee, Mistress Page – at the least if the love of soldier
can suffice – that I love thee. I will not say, pity me – 'tis not a
soldier-like phrase – but I say, love me. By me,
Thine own true knight,
By day or night,
Or any kind of light,
With all his might,
For thee to fight,
John Falstaff.
What a Herod of Jewry is this! O wicked, wicked world!
One that is well-nigh worn to pieces with age to show
himself a young gallant! What an unweighed behaviour

hath this Flemish drunkard picked – with the devil's name! – out of my conversation, that he dares in this manner assay me? Why, he hath not been thrice in my company. What should I say to him? I was then frugal of my mirth – heaven forgive me! Why, I'll exhibit a bill in the parliament for the putting down of men. How shall I be revenged on him? For revenged I will be, as sure as his guts are made of puddings.

[III, iii, 44–80] *And the other object of his ardour and eloquence, it seems, is anything but convinced – with a warning in her conclusion, if he cared to listen:*

FALSTAFF
Mistress Ford, I cannot cog, I cannot prate, Mistress Ford. Now shall I sin in my wish: I would thy husband were dead. I'll speak it before the best lord, I would make thee my lady.

MRS FORD
I your lady, Sir John? Alas, I should be a pitiful lady.

FALSTAFF
Let the court of France show me such another. I see how thine eye would emulate the diamond. Thou hast the right arched beauty of the brow that becomes the ship-tire, the tire-valiant, or any tire of Venetian admittance.

MRS FORD
A plain kerchief, Sir John. My brows become nothing else, nor that well neither.

FALSTAFF
Thou art a tyrant to say so. Thou wouldst make an

absolute courtier, and the firm fixture of thy foot would give an excellent motion to thy gait in a semi-circled farthingale. I see what thou wert, if Fortune, thy foe, were – not Nature – thy friend. Come, thou canst not hide it.

MRS FORD
Believe me, there's no such thing in me.

FALSTAFF
What made me love thee? Let that persuade thee there's something extra ordinary in thee. Come, I cannot cog and say thou art this and that, like a many of these lisping hawthorn-buds that come like women in men's apparel, and smell like Bucklersbury in simple time. I cannot. But I love thee, none but thee; and thou deservest it.

MRS FORD
Do not betray me, sir. I fear you love Mistress Page.

FALSTAFF
Thou mightst as well say I love to walk by the Counter-gate, which is as hateful to me as the reek of a lime-kiln.

MRS FORD
Well, heaven knows how I love you. And you shall one day find it.

FALSTAFF
Keep in that mind – I'll deserve it.

MRS FORD
Nay, I must tell you, so you do, or else I could not be in that mind.

Much Ado About Nothing

[I, i, 220–47] Too clever, and far too proud, to abase himself before any woman, Benedick tells Don Pedro that he dares love to do its worst:

BENEDICK

That a woman conceived me, I thank her; that she brought me up, I likewise give her most humble thanks; but that I will have a recheat winded in my forehead, or hang my bugle in an invisible baldrick, all women shall pardon me. Because I will not do them the wrong to mistrust any, I will do myself the right to trust none; and the fine is, for the which I may go the finer, I will live a bachelor.

DON PEDRO

I shall see thee, ere I die, look pale with love.

BENEDICK

With anger, with sickness, or with hunger, my lord, not with love. Prove that ever I lose more blood with love than I will get again with drinking, pick out mine eyes with a ballad-maker's pen and hang me up at the door of a brothel-house for the sign of blind Cupid.

DON PEDRO

Well, if ever thou dost fall from this faith, thou wilt prove a notable argument.

BENEDICK

If I do, hang me in a bottle like a cat, and shoot at me;
and he that hits me, let him be clapped on the shoulder,
and called Adam.

DON PEDRO

Well, as time shall try:
'In time the savage bull doth bear the yoke.'

BENEDICK

The savage bull may; but if ever the sensible Benedick
bear it, pluck off the bull's horns and set them in my
forehead, and let me be vilely painted; and in such great
letters as they write 'Here is good horse to hire', let them
signify under my sign 'Here you may see Benedick the
married man.'

[II, iii, 8–33] *Benedick marvels at the change wrought by love
for Hero in his old friend Claudio – the man's man par
excellence, he would have said. It will take an extraordinary
woman indeed to make such a fool of* him:

I do much wonder that one man, seeing how much
another man is a fool when he dedicates his behaviours
to love, will, after he hath laughed at such shallow follies
in others, become the argument of his own scorn by
falling in love; and such a man is Claudio. I have known
when there was no music with him but the drum and
the fife, and now had he rather hear the tabor and the
pipe. I have known when he would have walked ten
mile afoot to see a good armour; and now will he lie ten
nights awake carving the fashion of a new doublet. He

was wont to speak plain and to the purpose, like an honest man and a soldier, and now is he turned orthography; his words are a very fantastical banquet, just so many strange dishes. May I be so converted and see with these eyes? I cannot tell; I think not. I will not be sworn but love may transform me to an oyster; but I'll take my oath on it, till he have made an oyster of me, he shall never make me such a fool. One woman is fair, yet I am well; another is wise, yet I am well; another virtuous, yet I am well; but till all graces be in one woman, one woman shall not come in my grace. Rich she shall be, that's certain; wise, or I'll none; virtuous, or I'll never cheapen her; fair, or I'll never look on her; mild, or come not near me; noble, or not I for an angel; of good discourse, an excellent musician, and her hair shall be of what colour it please God.

Henry V

[V, ii, 122–66; 218–43] In his self-consciously rough-hewn soldier's style (including some early examples of 'franglais'), Henry V undertakes his wooing of the French Princess Katherine:

. . . I'faith, Kate, my wooing is fit for thy understanding. I am glad thou canst speak no better English; for if thou couldst, thou wouldst find me such a plain king that thou wouldst think I had sold my farm to buy my crown. I know no ways to mince it in love, but directly to say 'I love you': then if you urge me farther than to say, 'Do you in faith?' I wear out my suit. Give me your answer; i' faith, do; and so clap hands, and a bargain. How say you, lady?

KATHERINE
Sauf votre honneur, me understand well.

KING HENRY
Marry, if you would put me to verses, or to dance for your sake, Kate, why, you undid me. For the one, I have neither words nor measure; and for the other I have no strength in measure, yet a reasonable measure in strength. If I could win a lady at leap-frog, or by vaulting into my saddle with my armour on my back, under the correction of bragging be it spoken, I should quickly leap into wife. Or if I might buffet for my love, or bound my

horse for her favours, I could lay on like a butcher, and
sit like a jack an apes, never off. But, before God, Kate, I
cannot look greenly, nor gasp out my cloquence, nor I
have no cunning in protestation: only downright oaths,
which I never use till urged, nor never break for urging.
If thou canst love a fellow of this temper, Kate, whose
face is not worth sunburning, that never looks in his
glass for love of anything he sees there, let thine eye be
thy cook. I speak to thee plain soldier. If thou canst love
me for this, take me; if not, to say to thee that I shall die
is true – but for thy love, by the Lord, no – yet I love
thee too. And while thou liv'st, dear Kate, take a fellow
of plain and uncoined constancy; for he perforce must do
thee right, because he hath not the gift to woo in other
places. For these fellows of infinite tongue, that can
rhyme themselves into ladies' favours, they do always
reason themselves out again. What! A speaker is but a
prater, a rhyme is but a ballad. A good leg will fall; a
straight back will stoop; a black beard will turn white; a
curled pate will grow bald; a fair face will wither; a full
eye will wax hollow: but a good heart, Kate, is the sun
and the moon; or, rather, the sun, and not the moon; for
it shines bright and never changes, but keeps his course
truly. If thou would have such a one, take me; and take
me, take a soldier; take a soldier, take a king. And what
say'st thou then to my love? . . .

. . . By mine honour, in true English, I love thee, Kate; by
which honour I dare not swear thou lovest me, yet my
blood begins to flatter me that thou dost,
notwithstanding the poor and untempering effect of my

visage. Now beshrew my father's ambition! He was thinking of civil wars when he got me; therefore was I created with a stubborn outside, with an aspect of iron, that when I come to woo ladies I fright them. But in faith, Kate, the elder I wax, the better I shall appear. My comfort is, that old age, that ill layer-up of beauty, can do no more spoil upon my face. Thou hast me, if thou hast me, at the worst; and thou shalt wear me, if thou wear me, better and better; and therefore tell me, most fair Katherine, will you have me? Put off your maiden blushes, avouch the thoughts of your heart with the looks of an empress, take me by the hand, and say, 'Harry of England, I am thine': which word thou shalt no sooner bless mine ear withal but I will tell thee aloud 'England is thine, Ireland is thine, France is thine, and Henry Plantagenet is thine' – who, though I speak it before his face, if he be not fellow with the best king, thou shalt find the best king of good fellows. Come, your answer in broken music – for thy voice is music, and thy English broken; therefore, Queen of all, Katherine, break thy mind to me in broken English – wilt thou have me?

Julius Caesar

[II, i, 261–87] *Anxious and on edge as his conspiracy against Caesar gathers momentum, Brutus has taken to pacing up and down in his orchard late at night. Here, at last, he is confronted by his loving and loyal wife Portia, who feels he is murdering their marriage with his lack of frankness:*

Is Brutus sick? And is it physical
To walk unbracèd and suck up the humours
Of the dank morning? What, is Brutus sick?
And will he steal out of his wholesome bed
To dare the vile contagion of the night,
And tempt the rheumy, and unpurgèd air,
To add unto his sickness? No, my Brutus;
You have some sick offence within your mind,
Which, by the right and virtue of my place,
I ought to know of: and, upon my knees,
I charm you, by my once commended beauty,
By all your vows of Love, and that great vow
Which did incorporate and make us one,
That you unfold to me, your self, your half,
Why you are heavy, and what men tonight
Have had resort to you; for here have been
Some six or seven, who did hide their faces
Even from darkness.

BRUTUS

Kneel not, gentle Portia.

PORTIA

I should not need, if you were gentle Brutus.
Within the bond of marriage, tell me, Brutus,
Is it excepted I should know no secrets
That appertain to you? Am I your self,
But, as it were, in sort or limitation,
To keep with you at meals, comfort your bed,
And talk to you sometimes? Dwell I but in the suburbs
Of your good pleasure? If it be no more,
Portia is Brutus' Harlot, not his wife.

As You Like It

[II, iv, 19–51] *Shepherds Corin and Silvius represent age and youth in conversation and (on Silvius' side at any rate) competition. Rosalind and Touchstone the clown overhear – how comforting Silvius would find the latter's sympathetic recollections must be doubtful:*

SILVIUS

O Corin, that thou knewest how I do love her!

CORIN

I partly guess, for I have loved ere now.

SILVIUS

No, Corin, being old, thou canst not guess,
Though in thy youth thou wast as true a lover
As ever sighed upon a midnight pillow.
But if thy love were ever like to mine –
As sure I think did never man love so –
How many actions most ridiculous
Hast thou been drawn to by thy fantasy?

CORIN

Into a thousand that I have forgotten.

SILVIUS

O, thou didst then never love so heartily.
If thou rememberest not the slightest folly
That ever love did make thee run into,
Thou hast not loved.

Or if thou hast not sat as I do now,
Wearing thy hearer in thy mistress' praise,
Thou hast not loved.
Or if thou hast not broke from company
Abruptly, as my passion now makes me,
Thou hast not loved.
O Phebe, Phebe, Phebe!   *Exit* Silvius

ROSALIND
Alas, poor shepherd, searching of thy wound,
I have by hard adventure found mine own.

TOUCHSTONE
And I mine. I remember, when I was in love, I broke my
sword upon a stone and bid him take that for coming
a-night to Jane Smile, and I remember the kissing of her
batler and the cow's dugs that her pretty chopt hands
had milked; and I remember the wooing of a peascod
instead of her, from whom I took two cods and, giving
her them again, said with weeping tears, 'Wear these for
my sake.' We that are true lovers run into strange
capers; but as all is mortal in nature, so is all nature in
love mortal in folly.

[III, ii, 84–112] *Wandering the woods with Touchstone,
Rosalind has mixed feelings on finding herself immortalized in
doggerel scripts pinned to every tree:*

*From the east to western Ind,
No jewel is like Rosalind.
Her worth, being mounted on the wind,
Through all the world bears Rosalind.*

All the pictures fairest lined
Are but black to Rosalind.
Let no face be kept in mind
But the fair of Rosalind.

TOUCHSTONE

I'll rhyme you so eight years together, dinners
and suppers and sleeping hours excepted: it is the right
butter-women's rank to market.

ROSALIND

Out, fool!

TOUCHSTONE

For a taste:
If a hart do lack a hind,
Let him seek out Rosalind.
If the cat will after kind,
So be sure will Rosalind.
Winter garments must be lined,
So must slender Rosalind.
They that reap must sheaf and bind,
Then to cart with Rosalind.
Sweetest nut hath sourest rind,
Such a nut is Rosalind.
He that sweetest rose will find,
Must find love's prick and Rosalind.
This is the very false gallop of verses. Why do you infect
yourself with them?

ROSALIND

Peace, you dull fool, I found them on a tree.

TOUCHSTONE

Truly, the tree yields bad fruit.

ORLANDO

Are you native of this place?

ROSALIND

As the coney that you see dwell where she is kindled.

ORLANDO

Your accent is something finer than you could purchase
in so removed a dwelling.

ROSALIND

I have been told so of many; but indeed an old religious
uncle of mine taught me to speak, who was in his youth
an inland man – one that knew courtship too well, for
there he fell in love. I have heard him read many lectures
against it, and I thank God I am not a woman, to be
touched with so many giddy offences as he hath
generally taxed their whole sex withal.

ORLANDO

Can you remember any of the principal evils that he laid
to the charge of women?

ROSALIND

There were none principal, they were all like one
another as halfpence are, every one fault seeming
monstrous till his fellow-fault came to match it.

ORLANDO

I prithee, recount some of them.

ROSALIND

No, I will not cast away my physic but on those that are
sick. There is a man haunts the forest that abuses our
young plants with carving 'Rosalind' on their barks;

hangs odes upon hawthorns, and elegies on brambles; all, forsooth, deifying the name of Rosalind. If I could meet that fancy-monger, I would give him some good counsel, for he seems to have the quotidian of love upon him.

ORLANDO

I am he that is so love-shaked. I pray you, tell me your remedy.

ROSALIND

There is none of my uncle's marks upon you. He taught me how to know a man in love; in which cage of rushes I am sure you are not prisoner.

ORLANDO

What were his marks?

ROSALIND

A lean cheek, which you have not; a blue eye and sunken, which you have not; an unquestionable spirit, which you have not; a beard neglected, which you have not – but I pardon you for that, for simply your having in beard is a younger brother's revenue. Then your hose should be ungartered, your bonnet unbanded, your sleeve unbuttoned, your shoe untied, and every thing about you demonstrating a careless desolation. But you are no such man: you are rather point-device in your accoutrements, as loving yourself, than seeming the lover of any other.

ORLANDO

Fair youth, I would I could make thee believe I love.

ROSALIND

Me believe it! You may as soon make her that you love believe it, which I warrant she is apter to do than to

confess she does: that is one of the points in the which
women still give the lie to their consciences. But in good
sooth, are you he that hangs the verses on the trees,
wherein Rosalind is so admired?

ORLANDO
I swear to thee, youth, by the white hand of Rosalind, I
am that he, that unfortunate he.

ROSALIND
But are you so much in love as your rhymes speak?

ORLANDO
Neither rhyme nor reason can express how much.

ROSALIND
Love is merely a madness and, I tell you, deserves as well
a dark house and a whip as madmen do; and the reason
why they are not so punished and cured is that the
lunacy is so ordinary that the whippers are in love too.

[III, v, 1–27] *A shepherdess commits the cardinal cruelty of*
affecting to take her swain's protestations literally:

SILVIUS
Sweet Phebe, do not scorn me, do not, Phebe.
Say that you love me not, but say not so
In bitterness. The common executioner,
Whose heart th' accustomed sight of death makes hard,
Falls not the axe upon the humbled neck
But first begs pardon: will you sterner be
Than he that dies and lives by bloody drops?
    Enter Rosalind, Celia and Corin, unobserved

PHEBE

I would not be thy executioner.
I fly thee, for I would not injure thee.
Thou tellest me there is murder in mine eye:
'Tis pretty, sure, and very probable,
That eyes, that are the frail'st and softest things,
Who shut their coward gates on atomies,
Should be called tyrants, butchers, murderers!
Now I do frown on thee with all my heart,
And if mine eyes can wound, now let them kill thee.
Now counterfeit to swoon, why now fall down,
Or, if thou canst not, O, for shame, for shame,
Lie not, to say mine eyes are murderers!
Now show the wound mine eye hath made in thee.
Scratch thee but with a pin, and there remains
Some scar of it; lean upon a rush,
The cicatrice and capable impressure
Thy palm some moment keeps; but now mine eyes,
Which I have darted at thee, hurt thee not;
Nor, I am sure, there is not force in eyes
That can do hurt.

[IV, i, 85–98] *But Rosalind is sceptical in her turn about*
Orlando's claims that he might die for love:

. . . The poor world is almost six thousand years old,
and in all this time there was not any man died in his
own person, videlicet, in a love-cause. Troilus had his
brains dashed out with a Grecian club, yet he did what
he could to die before, and he is one of the patterns of

love. Leander, he would have lived many a fair year though Hero had turned nun, if it had not been for a hot midsummer night; for, good youth, he went but forth to wash him in the Hellespont and being taken with the cramp was drowned, and the foolish chroniclers of that age found it was 'Hero of Sestos'. But these are all lies; men have died from time to time and worms have eaten them, but not for love.

Hamlet

[I, iii, 110–20] *Polonius harrumphs away Hamlet's vows of love when his daughter tells him of them:*

OPHELIA
My lord, he hath importuned me with love
In honourable fashion.

POLONIUS
Ay, 'fashion' you may call it. Go to, go to.

OPHELIA
And hath given countenance to his speech, my lord,
With almost all the holy vows of heaven.

POLONIUS
Ay, springes to catch woodcocks. I do know,
When the blood burns, how prodigal the soul
Lends the tongue vows. These blazes, daughter,
Giving more light than heat, extinct in both
Even in their promise, as it is a-making,
You must not take for fire.

[II, ii, 115–18] *In a love letter to Ophelia, the young Prince breaks into verse:*

Doubt thou the stars are fire.
  Doubt that the sun doth move.

Doubt truth to be a liar.
  But never doubt I love.

[III, iv, 54–89] *His mother Gertrude married her brother-in-law within weeks of his father's death. Hamlet berates her not only for her disloyalty but for having sexual desires at all:*

Look here upon this picture, and on this,
The counterfeit presentment of two brothers.
See what a grace was seated on this brow:
Hyperion's curls, the front of Jove himself,
An eye like Mars, to threaten and command,
A station like the herald Mercury
New lighted on a heaven-kissing hill:
A combination and a form indeed
Where every god did seem to set his seal
To give the world assurance of a man.
This was your husband. Look you now what follows.
Here is your husband; like a mildewed ear,
Blasting his wholesome brother. Have you eyes?
Could you on this fair mountain leave to feed,
And batten on this moor? Ha! Have you eyes?
You cannot call it love. For at your age
The heyday in the blood is tame; it's humble,
And waits upon the judgment; and what judgment
Would step from this to this? Sense sure you have,
Else could you not have motion. But sure that sense
Is apoplexed. For madness would not err,
Nor sense to ecstacy was ne'er so thralled
But it reserved some quantity of choice

To serve in such a difference. What devil was't
That thus hath cozened you at hoodman-blind?
Eyes without feeling, feeling without sight,
Ears without hands or eyes, smelling sans all,
Or but a sickly part of one true sense
Could not so mope.
O shame, where is thy blush? Rebellious hell,
If thou canst mutine in a matron's bones,
To flaming youth let virtue be as wax
And melt in her own fire. Proclaim no shame
When the compulsive ardour gives the charge,
Since frost itself as actively doth burn,
And reason panders will.

Twelfth Night

[I, i, 1–15] *Orsino, Duke of Illyria, is made restless by unrequited love:*

If music be the food of love, play on,
Give me excess of it, that, surfeiting,
The appetite may sicken, and so die.
That strain again! It had a dying fall.
O, it came o'er my ear like the sweet sound
That breathes upon a bank of violets,
Stealing and giving odour. Enough, no more!
'Tis not so sweet now as it was before.
O spirit of love, how quick and fresh art thou,
That, notwithstanding thy capacity
Receiveth as the sea, nought enters there,
Of what validity and pitch soe'er,
But falls into abatement and low price
Even in a minute. So full of shapes is fancy
That it alone is high fantastical.

[II, iv, 78–117] *Disguised as a boy called Cesario, Viola is able*
to put in a good word for women – for love, it seems, has left
Orsino in misogynistic mood:

. . . Once more, Cesario,
Get thee to yond same sovereign cruelty.
Tell her my love, more noble than the world,
Prizes not quantity of dirty lands;
The parts that fortune hath bestowed upon her
Tell her I hold as giddily as fortune.
But 'tis that miracle and queen of gems
That nature pranks her in, attracts my soul.

VIOLA

But if she cannot love you, sir?

DUKE

It cannot be so answered.

VIOLA

Sooth, but you must.
Say that some lady, as perhaps there is,
Hath for your love as great a pang of heart
As you have for Olivia. You cannot love her.
You tell her so. Must she not then be answered?

DUKE

There is no woman's sides
Can bide the beating of so strong a passion
As love doth give my heart; no woman's heart
So big to hold so much, they lack retention.
Alas, their love may be called appetite,
No motion of the liver, but the palate,
That suffer surfeit, cloyment, and revolt.
But mine is all as hungry as the sea,

And can digest as much. Make no compare
Between that love a woman can bear me
And that I owe Olivia.

VIOLA

Ay, but I know –

DUKE

What dost thou know?

VIOLA

Too well what love women to men may owe.
In faith, they are as true of heart as we.
My father had a daughter loved a man –
As it might be perhaps, were I a woman,
I should your lordship.

DUKE

And what's her history?

VIOLA

A blank, my lord. She never told her love,
But let concealment, like a worm i' the bud,
Feed on her damask cheek. She pined in thought,
And with a green and yellow melancholy,
She sat like Patience on a monument,
Smiling at grief. Was not this love indeed?
We men may say more, swear more, but indeed
Our shows are more than will; for still we prove
Much in our vows, but little in our love.

Troilus and Cressida

[I, i, 91–106] *Prince Troilus has bigger things on his mind than the War of Troy: the beauties of Cressida – and his exasperation with the messenger of his devotion, Lord Pandarus:*

Peace, you ungracious clamours! Peace, rude sounds!
Fools on both sides! Helen must needs be fair,
When with your blood you daily paint her thus.
I cannot fight upon this argument;
It is too starved a subject for my sword.
But Pandarus – O gods, how do you plague me!
I cannot come to Cressid but by Pandar,
And he's as tetchy to be wooed to woo
As she is stubborn-chaste against all suit.
Tell me, Apollo, for thy Daphne's love,
What Cressid is, what Pandar, and what we –
Her bed is India; there she lies, a pearl:
Between our Ilium and where she resides
Let it be called the wild and wandering flood,
Ourself the merchant, and this sailing Pandar
Our doubtful hope, our convoy, and our bark.

[I, ii, 282–95] *Cressida too finds romance by proxy hard, but knows better than to give any ground. Once she does, she knows, her power over Troilus will be diminished:*

Words, vows, gifts, tears, and love's full sacrifice
He offers in another's enterprise;
But more in Troilus thousandfold I see
Than in the glass of Pandar's praise may be.
Yet hold I off. Women are angels, wooing;
Things won are done; joy's soul lies in the doing.
That she beloved knows naught that knows not this:
Men prize the thing ungained more than it is.
That she was never yet that ever knew
Love got so sweet as when desire did sue;
Therefore this maxim out of love I teach:
'Achievement is command; ungained, beseech.'
Then, though my heart's content firm love doth bear,
Nothing of that shall from mine eyes appear.

[III, ii, 16–27] *As he waits to meet in person the woman he has so long loved from afar, Troilus is not sure he will be able to cope with the ecstasy:*

I am giddy; expectation whirls me round.
Th' imaginary relish is so sweet
That it enchants my sense. What will it be,
When that the watery palate tastes indeed
Love's thrice-repurèd nectar? – death, I fear me,
Swooning destruction, or some joy too fine,
Too subtle-potent, tuned too sharp in sweetness,

For the capacity of my ruder powers.
I fear it much; and I do fear besides
That I shall lose distinction in my joys,
As doth a battle, when they charge on heaps
The enemy flying.

[III, ii, 60–95] *Pandarus having brought Cressida to Troilus,
the lovers are alone together at last. Troilus cannot believe his
good fortune; Cressida's incredulity seems a little more literal
and far-reaching:*

TROILUS
O Cressid, how often have I wished me thus!

CRESSIDA
Wished, my lord! – The gods grant – O my lord!

TROILUS
What should they grant? What makes this pretty
abruption? What too curious dreg espies my sweet lady
in the fountain of our love?

CRESSIDA
More dregs than water, if my fears have eyes.

TROILUS
Fears make devils of cherubins; they never see truly.

CRESSIDA
Blind fear, that seeing reason leads, finds safer footing
than blind reason stumbling without fear: to fear the
worst oft cures the worst.

TROILUS
O, let my lady apprehend no fear; in all Cupid's pageant
there is presented no monster.

CRESSIDA

Nor nothing monstrous neither?

TROILUS

Nothing, but our undertakings when we vow to weep
seas, live in fire, eat rocks, tame tigers; thinking it harder
for our mistress to devise imposition enough than for us
to undergo any difficulty imposed. This is the
monstruosity in love, lady, that the will is infinite, and
the execution confined; that the desire is boundless, and
the act a slave to limit.

CRESSIDA

They say all lovers swear more performance than they
are able, and yet reserve an ability that they never
perform; vowing more than the perfection of ten, and
discharging less than the tenth part of one. They that
have the voice of lions and the act of hares, are they not
monsters?

TROILUS

Are there such? Such are not we. Praise us as we are
tasted, allow us as we prove. Our head shall go bare till
merit crown it; no perfection in reversion shall have a
praise in present. We will not name desert before his
birth, and, being born, his addition shall be humble: few
words to fair faith. Troilus shall be such to Cressid as
what envy can say worst shall be a mock for his truth,
and what truth can speak truest, not truer than Troilus.

[III, ii, 111–209] *With Pandarus presiding, Troilus and Cressida exchange their vows in a mock-marriage. This most affecting of scenes is, unfortunately, charged to the full with irony, since Cressida will before too long be finding herself another lover:*

CRESSIDA
Boldness comes to me now, and brings me heart:
Prince Troilus, I have loved you night and day
For many weary months.

TROILUS
Why was my Cressid then so hard to win?

CRESSIDA
Hard to seem won; but I was won, my lord;
With the first glance that ever – pardon me.
If I confess much, you will play the tyrant.
I love you now; but till now not so much
But I might master it. In faith, I lie;
My thoughts were like unbridled children, grown
Too headstrong for their mother – see, we fools!
Why have I blabbed? Who shall be true to us
When we are so unsecret to ourselves? –
But though I loved you well, I wooed you not;
And yet, good faith, I wished myself a man,
Or that we women had men's privilege
Of speaking first. Sweet, bid me hold my tongue,
For in this rapture I shall surely speak
The thing I shall repent. See, see, your silence,
Cunning in dumbness, from my weakness draws
My soul of counsel from me! – Stop my mouth.

TROILUS

And shall, albeit sweet music issues thence.

He kisses her

PANDARUS

Pretty, i' faith.

CRESSIDA

My lord, I do beseech you, pardon me;
'Twas not my purpose thus to beg a kiss.
I am ashamed. O heavens, what have I done?
For this time will I take my leave, my lord.

TROILUS

Your leave, sweet Cressid!

PANDARUS

Leave? An you take leave till tomorrow morning –

CRESSIDA

Pray you, content you.

TROILUS

                  What offends you, lady?

CRESSIDA

Sir, mine own company.

TROILUS

                  You cannot shun yourself.

CRESSIDA

Let me go and try.
I have a kind of self resides with you;
But an unkind self, that itself will leave
To be another's fool. Where is my wit?
I would be gone; I speak I know not what.

TROILUS

Well know they what they speak that speak so wisely.

CRESSIDA

Perchance, my lord, I showed more craft than love,
And fell so roundly to a large confession,
To angle for your thoughts; but you are wise,
Or else you love not; for to be wise and love
Exceeds man's might – that dwells with gods above.

TROILUS

O that I thought it could be in a woman –
As, if it can, I will presume in you –
To feed for aye her lamp and flames of love;
To keep her constancy in plight and youth,
Outliving beauty's outward, with a mind
That doth renew swifter than blood decays!
Or that persuasion could but thus convince me,
That my integrity and truth to you
Might be affronted with the match and weight
Of such a winnowed purity in love –
How were I then uplifted! But alas,
I am as true as truth's simplicity,
And simpler than the infancy of truth.

CRESSIDA

In that I'll war with you.

TROILUS

                              O virtuous fight,
When right with right wars who shall be most right!
True swains in love shall in the world to come
Approve their truth by Troilus, when their rhymes,
Full of protest, of oath, and big compare,
Want similes, truth tired with iteration –
As true as steel, as plantage to the moon,

As sun to day, as turtle to her mate,
As iron to adamant, as earth to th' centre –
Yet, after all comparisons of truth,
As truth's authentic author to be cited,
'As true as Troilus' shall crown up the verse,
And sanctify the numbers.

CRESSIDA

                              Prophet may you be!
If I be false, or swerve a hair from truth,
When time is old and hath forgot itself,
When waterdrops have worn the stones of Troy,
And blind oblivion swallowed cities up,
And mighty states characterless are grated
To dusty nothing; yet let memory,
From false to false, among false maids in love,
Upbraid my falsehood! When they've said 'As false
As air, as water, wind, or sandy earth,
As fox to lamb, or wolf to heifer's calf,
Pard to the hind, or stepdame to her son' –
Yea, let them say, to stick the heart of falsehood,
'As false as Cressid.'

PANDARUS

Go to, a bargain made; seal it, seal it, I'll be the witness.
Here I hold your hand, here my cousin's. If ever you
prove false one to another, since I have taken such pains
to bring you together, let all pitiful goers-between be
called to the world's end after my name, call them all
Pandars. Let all constant men be Troiluses, all false
women Cressids, and all brokers between Pandars!
Say 'Amen.'

TROILUS
Amen.

CRESSIDA
Amen.

PANDARUS
Amen. Whereupon I will show you a chamber with a
bed; which bed, because it shall not speak of your pretty
encounters, press it to death: away! –

Exeunt Troilus and Cressida

And Cupid grant all tongue-tied maidens here,
Bed, chamber, and Pandar to provide this gear!

Measure for Measure

[II, ii, 163–88] *Angelo wonders if Isabella's chastity might not be inflammatory in itself:*

What's this, what's this? Is this her fault or mine?
The tempter, or the tempted, who sins most?
Ha?
Not she, nor doth she tempt; but it is I
That, lying by the violet in the sun,
Do as the carrion does, not as the flower,
Corrupt with virtuous season. Can it be
That modesty may more betray our sense
Than woman's lightness? Having waste ground enough,
Shall we desire to raze the sanctuary
And pitch our evils there? O, fie, fie, fie!
What dost thou? Or what art thou, Angelo?
Dost thou desire her foully for those things
That make her good? O, let her brother live:
Thieves for their robbery have authority
When judges steal themselves. What, do I love her,
That I desire to hear her speak again,
And feast upon her eyes? What is't I dream on?
O cunning enemy that, to catch a saint,
With saints dost bait thy hook. Most dangerous
Is that temptation that doth goad us on
To sin in loving virtue. Never could the strumpet

With all her double vigour, art and nature,
Once stir my temper; but this virtuous maid
Subdues me quite. Ever till now,
When men were fond, I smiled and wondered how.

[II, iv, 19–29] *Always sober and self-righteously celibate,*
Angelo is shocked by his feelings for the beautiful and virtuous
Isabella:

... O heavens,
Why does my blood thus muster to my heart,
Making both it unable for itself,
And dispossessing all my other parts
Of necessary fitness?
So play the foolish throngs with one that swoons,
Come all to help him, and so stop the air
By which he should revive; and even so
The general, subject to a well-wished king,
Quit their own part, and in obsequious fondness
Crowd to his presence, where their untaught love
Must needs appear offence.

[IV, i, 1–6] *Angelo's abandoned love, Mariana, sings a song of*
sad resignation – as yet unaware that he will have to honour
his contract by the action's end:

Take, O take those lips away
That so sweetly were forsworn;
And those eyes, the break of day,

Lights that do mislead the morn:
But my kisses bring again, bring again;
Seals of love, but sealed in vain, sealed in vain.

Othello

The Moor Othello responds to Brabantio's charge that he ensnared his daughter Desdemona by means of 'sorcery':

Her father loved me, oft invited me,
Still questioned me the story of my life
From year to year – the battles, sieges, fortunes
That I have passed.
I ran it through, even from my boyish days
To th'very moment that he bade me tell it:
Wherein I spake of most disastrous chances,
Of moving accidents by flood and field,
Of hair-breadth scapes i'th'imminent deadly breach,
Of being taken by the insolent foe,
And sold to slavery; of my redemption thence,
And portance in my travels' history:
Wherein of antres vast and deserts idle,
Rough quarries, rocks, and hills whose heads touch
    heaven,
It was my hint to speak – such was the process:
And of the Cannibals that each other eat,
The Anthropophagi, and men whose heads
Do grow beneath their shoulders. This to hear
Would Desdemona seriously incline:
But still the house affairs would draw her thence,

Which ever as she could with haste dispatch
She'd come again, and with a greedy ear
Devour up my discourse; which I observing
Took once a pliant hour, and found good means
To draw from her a prayer of earnest heart
That I would all my pilgrimage dilate
Whereof by parcels she had something heard,
But not intentively. I did consent,
And often did beguile her of her tears
When I did speak of some distressful stroke
That my youth suffered. My story being done,
She gave me for my pains a world of sighs:
She swore, in faith 'twas strange, 'twas passing strange,
'Twas pitiful, 'twas wondrous pitiful;
She wished she had not heard it, yet she wished
That heaven had made her such a man. She thanked me,
And bade me, if I had a friend that loved her,
I should but teach him how to tell my story,
And that would woo her. Upon this hint I spake:
She loved me for the dangers I had passed,
And I loved her, that she did pity them.
This only is the witchcraft I have used.

[I, iii, 245–56] *Desdemona, asked by the Duke for her view,
makes it clear that she loves her husband more for his mind
and body than his biography:*

That I did love the Moor to live with him,
My downright violence and storm of fortunes
May trumpet to the world. My heart's subdued

Even to the very quality of my lord.
I saw Othello's visage in his mind
And to his honors and his valiant parts
Did I my soul and fortunes consecrate.
So that, dear lords, if I be left behind
A moth of peace, and he go to the war,
The rites for which I love him are bereft me,
And I a heavy interim shall support
By his dear absence. Let me go with him.

[III, iii, 255–270] *Othello, in his jealousy, is only too ready to credit his ensign Iago's wicked insinuations – that Desdemona is no true falcon but a faithless 'haggard' hawk:*

This fellow's of exceeding honesty,
And knows all qualities with a learnèd spirit
Of human dealings. If I do prove her haggard,
Though that her jesses were my dear heart-strings,
I'd whistle her off, and let her down the wind
To prey at fortune. Haply, for I am black
And have not those soft parts of conversation
That chamberers have; or for I am declined
Into the vale of years – yet that's not much –
She's gone: I am abused, and my relief
Must be to loathe her. O, curse of marriage!
That we can call these delicate creatures ours
And not their appetites! I had rather be a toad
And live upon the vapor of a dungeon
Than keep a corner in the thing I love
For others' uses . . .

*Packed off to bed by her angry husband,
Desdemona talks men and fidelity with her maid, Emilia, and
finds the age-old mysteries of love are perhaps best captured in
a folksong she recalls:*

He hath commanded me to go to bed,
And bade me to dismiss you.

EMILIA

                                    Dismiss me?

DESDEMONA

It was his bidding; therefore, good Emilia,
Give me my nightly wearing, and adieu.
We must not now displease him.

EMILIA

I would you had never seen him!

DESDEMONA

So would not I: my love doth so approve him
That even his stubbornness, his checks, his frowns –
Prithee, unpin me – have grace and favor in them.

EMILIA

I have laid those sheets you bade me, on the bed.

DESDEMONA

All's one. Good faith, how foolish are our minds!
If I do die before thee, prithee shroud me
In one of those same sheets.

EMILIA

                                    Come, come, you talk.

DESDEMONA

My mother had a maid called Barbary:
She was in love: and he she loved proved mad
And did forsake her. She had a song of willow;

An old thing 'twas; but it expressed her fortune,
And she died singing it. That song tonight
Will not go from my mind: I have much to do
But to go hang my head all at one side
And sing it like poor Barbary – prithee, dispatch . . .
　　(*She sings*)
The poor soul sat sighing by a sycamore tree,
　　Sing all a green willow;
Her hand on her bosom, her head on her knee,
　　Sing willow, willow, willow;
The fresh streams ran by her, and murmured her moans;
　　Sing willow, willow, willow;
Her salt tears fell from her, and softened the stones –
　　(*She speaks*)
Lay by these.
　　(*She sings*)
Sing willow, willow, willow –
　　(*She speaks*)
Prithee, hie thee; he'll come anon.
　　(*She sings*)
Sing all a green willow must be my garland.
Let nobody blame him; his scorn I approve –
　　(*She speaks*)
Nay, that's not next. Hark, who is't that knocks?

EMILIA

It's the wind.

DESDEMONA (*sings*)

I called my love false love, but what said he then?
　　Sing willow, willow, willow:
If I court moe women, you'll couch with moe men.
　　(*She speaks*)

So get thee gone; good night. Mine eyes do itch:
Does that bode weeping?

EMILIA

                        'Tis neither here nor there.

DESDEMONA

I have heard it said so. O, these men, these men!
Dost thou in conscience think – tell me, Emilia –
That there be women do abuse their husbands
In such gross kind?

EMILIA

                There be some such, no question.

DESDEMONA

Wouldst thou do such a deed for all the world?

EMILIA

Why, would not you?

DESDEMONA

              No, by this heavenly light.

EMILIA

Nor I neither by this heavenly light: I might do't as well
i'th'dark.

DESDEMONA

Wouldst thou do such a deed for all the world?

EMILIA

The world's a huge thing: it is a great price for a small
vice.

DESDEMONA

In troth, I think thou wouldst not.

EMILIA

In troth I think I should, and undo't when I had done it.
Marry, I would not do such a thing for a joint ring, nor
for measures of lawn, nor for gowns, petticoats, nor

caps, nor any petty exhibition. But for the whole world!
Ud's pity, who would not make her husband a cuckold,
to make him a monarch? I should venture purgatory
for't.

DESDEMONA

Beshrew me, if I would do such a wrong for the whole
world.

EMILIA

Why, the wrong is but a wrong i'th'world; and having
the world for your labour, 'tis a wrong in your own
world, and you might quickly make it right.

DESDEMONA

I do not think there is any such woman.

EMILIA

Yes, a dozen: and as many to th'vantage as would store
the world they played for.
But I do think it is their husbands' faults
If wives do fall. Say that they slack their duties,
And pour our treasures into foreign laps;
Or else break out in peevish jealousies,
Throwing restraint upon us; or say they strike us,
Or scant our former having in despite –
Why, we have galls, and though we have some grace,
Yet have we some revenge. Let husbands know
Their wives have sense like them: they see and smell,
And have their palates both for sweet and sour
As husbands have. What is it that they do,
When they change us for others? Is it sport?
I think it is. And doth affection breed it?
I think it doth. Is't frailty that thus errs?
It is so too. And have not we affections,

Desires for sport, and frailty, as men have?
Then let them use us well: else let them know,
The ills we do, their ills instruct us so.

DESDEMONA
Good night, good night. God me such uses send,
Not to pick bad from bad, but by bad mend!

All's Well That Ends Well

[I, i, 78–97] *Helena feels guilty when people commiserate with her on her father's recent death: another, more violent, love has been monopolizing her emotions:*

O, were that all! I think not on my father,
And these great tears grace his remembrance more
Than those I shed for him. What was he like?
I have forgot him. My imagination
Carries no favour in't but Bertram's.
I am undone: there is no living, none,
If Bertram be away. 'Twere all one
That I should love a bright particular star
And think to wed it, he is so above me.
In his bright radiance and collateral light
Must I be comforted, not in his sphere.
Th' ambition in my love thus plagues itself:
The hind that would be mated by the lion
Must die for love. 'Twas pretty, though a plague,
To see him every hour, to sit and draw
His archèd brows, his hawking eye, his curls,
In our heart's table – heart too capable
Of every line and trick of his sweet favour.
But now he's gone, and my idolatrous fancy
Must sanctify his relics.

[I, iii, 190–212] *Helena acknowledges her hopeless passion to the Countess, her beloved's mother:*

My friends were poor; but honest; so's my love.
Be not offended, for it hurts not him
That he is loved of me. I follow him not
By any token of presumptuous suit,
Nor would I have him till I do deserve him,
Yet never know how that desert should be.
I know I love in vain, strive against hope,
Yet in this captious and intenable sieve
I still pour in the waters of my love
And lack not to lose still. Thus, Indian-like,
Religious in mine error, I adore
The sun that looks upon his worshipper
But knows of him no more. My dearest madam,
Let not your hate encounter with my love,
For loving where you do; but if yourself,
Whose aged honour cites a virtuous youth,
Did ever, in so true a flame of liking,
Wish chastely and love dearly that your Dian
Was both herself and love – O then, give pity
To her whose state is such that cannot choose
But lend and give where she is sure to lose;
That seeks not to find that her search implies,
But riddle-like lives sweetly where she dies.

Antony and Cleopatra

[I, i, 1–10] *Philo, a former comrade-at-arms, sees a sad transformation in Mark Antony:*

Nay, but this dotage of our general's
O'erflows the measure. Those his goodly eyes,
That o'er the files and musters of the war
Have glowed like plated Mars, now bend, now turn
The office and devotion of their view
Upon a tawny front. His captain's heart,
Which in the scuffles of great fights hath burst
The buckles on his breast, reneges all temper,
And is become the bellows and the fan
To cool a gipsy's lust.

*Flourish. Enter Antony, Cleopatra, her ladies Charmian
and Iras, the train, with eunuchs fanning her*
                        Look where they come.
Take but good note, and you shall see in him
The triple pillar of the world transformed
Into a strumpet's fool. Behold and see.

[I, i, 33–40] *Reproached by Cleopatra with what she says are his divided loyalties, Antony insists on the mad recklessness of his love for his Egyptian queen:*

Let Rome in Tiber melt, and the wide arch
Of the ranged empire fall! Here is my space.
Kingdoms are clay. Our dungy earth alike
Feeds beast as man. The nobleness of life
Is to do thus – when such a mutual pair
And such a twain can do't, in which I bind,
On pain of punishment, the world to weet
We stand up peerless.

[II, i, 20–26] *Pompey, one of Antony's rivals for power in Rome, permits himself the hope that Antony's Egyptian love will flourish – and continue to keep him from more manly aspirations:*

. . . But all the charms of love,
Salt Cleopatra, soften thy waned lip!
Let witchcraft join with beauty, lust with both!
Tie up the libertine in a field of feasts;
Keep his brain fuming. Epicurean cooks
Sharpen with cloyless sauce his appetite,
That sleep and feeding may prorogue his honour

[II, ii, 196–223] *Antony's servant Enobarbus recalls his
master's first meeting with Cleopatra, when she floated down
the Nile to make a conquest of the Roman conqueror:*

The barge she sat in, like a burnished throne,
Burned on the water. The poop was beaten gold;
Purple the sails, and so perfumèd that
The winds were lovesick with them. The oars were
    silver,
Which to the tune of flutes kept stroke, and made
The water which they beat to follow faster,
As amorous of their strokes. For her own person,
It beggared all description. She did lie
In her pavilion, cloth-of-gold, of tissue,
O'erpicturing that Venus where we see
The fancy outwork nature. On each side her
Stood pretty dimpled boys, like smiling cupids,
With divers-coloured fans, whose wind did seem
To glow the delicate cheeks which they did cool,
And what they undid did . . .
Her gentlewomen, like the Nereides,
So many mermaids, tended her i'th'eyes,
And made their bends adornings. At the helm
A seeming mermaid steers. The silken tackle
Swell with the touches of those flower-soft hands,
That yarely frame the office. From the barge
A strange invisible perfume hits the sense
Of the adjacent wharfs. The city cast
Her people out upon her; and Antony,
Enthroned i'th'market-place, did sit alone,
Whistling to th'air; which, but for vacancy,

Had gone to gaze on Cleopatra too,
And made a gap in nature.

[IV, xv, 72–90] *Nominally a queen, Cleopatra considers how
comprehensively she has been dethroned by love – and what is
left to her now an even mightier leveller, death, has taken
Antony:*

No more but e'en a woman, and commanded
By such poor passion as the maid that milks
And does the meanest chares. It were for me
To throw my sceptre at the injurious gods,
To tell them that this world did equal theirs
Till they had stolen our jewel. All's but naught.
Patience is sottish, and impatience does
Become a dog that's mad; then is it sin
To rush into the secret house of death
Ere death dare come to us? How do you, women?
What, what, good cheer! Why, how now, Charmian?
My noble girls! Ah, women, women, look,
Our lamp is spent, it's out. Good sirs, take heart.
We'll bury him; and then, what's brave, what's noble,
Let's do't after the high Roman fashion,
And make death proud to take us. Come, away.
This case of that huge spirit now is cold.
Ah, women, women! Come; we have no friend
But resolution, and the briefest end.

Cymbeline

[I, iii, 1–37] *Imogen quizzes Pisanio, wanting to hear every last detail of her husband Posthumus' departure:*

IMOGEN
I would thou grew'st unto the shores o' th' haven,
And questioned'st every sail; if he should write,
And I not have it, 'twere a paper lost,
As offer'd mercy is. What was the last
That he spake to thee?

PISANIO
                                    It was: his queen, his queen!

IMOGEN
Then wav'd his handkerchief?

PISANIO
                                    And kiss'd it, madam.

IMOGEN
Senseless linen, happier therein than I!
And that was all?

PISANIO
                        No, madam; for so long
As he could make me with his eye, or care
Distinguish him from others, he did keep
The deck, with glove, or hat, or handkerchief,
Still waving, as the fits and stirs of's mind
Could best express how slow his soul sail'd on,

How swift his ship.

IMOGEN

                    Thou shouldst have made him
As little as a crow, or less, ere left
To after-eye him.

PISANIO

                Madam, so I did.

IMOGEN

I would have broke mine eyestrings, crack'd them but
To look upon him, till the diminution
Of space had pointed him sharp as my needle;
Nay, followed him till he had melted from
The smallness of a gnat to air, and then
Have turn'd mine eye and wept. But, good Pisanio,
When shall we hear from him?

PISANIO

                     Be assur'd, madam,
With his next vantage.

IMOGEN

I did not take my leave of him, but had
Most pretty things to say. Ere I could tell him
How I would think on him at certain hours
Such thoughts and such; or I could make him swear
The shes of Italy should not betray
Mine interest and his honour; or have charg'd him,
At the sixth hour of morn, at noon, at midnight,
T'encounter me with orisons, for then
I am in heaven for him; or ere I could
Give him that parting kiss which I had set
Betwixt two charming words, comes in my father,

And like the tyrannous breathing of the north
Shakes all our buds from growing.

[II, v, 1–35] *News of Imogen's supposed infidelity has left*
Posthumus cursing womankind:

Is there no way for men to be, but women
Must be half-workers? We are all bastards,
And that most venerable man which I
Did call my father was I know not where
When I was stamp'd. Some coiner with his tools
Made me a counterfeit; yet my mother seem'd
The Dian of that time. So doth my wife
The nonpareil of this. O, vengeance, vengeance!
Me of my lawful pleasure she restrain'd,
And pray'd me oft forbearance; did it with
A pudency so rosy, the sweet view on't
Might well have warm'd old Saturn; that I thought her
As chaste as unsunn'd snow. O, all the devils!
... Could I find out
The woman's part in me! For there's no motion
That tends to vice in man but I affirm
It is the woman's part. Be it lying, note it,
The woman's; flattering, hers; deceiving, hers;
Lust and rank thoughts, hers, hers; revenges, hers;
Ambitions, covetings, change of prides, disdain,
Nice longing, slanders, mutability,
All faults that man may name, nay, that hell knows,
Why, hers, in part or all; but rather all;

For even to vice
They are not constant, but are changing still
One vice but of a minute old for one
Not half so old as that. I'll write against them,
Detest them, curse them. Yet 'tis greater skill
In a true hate to pray they have their will:
The very devils cannot plague them better.

The Tempest

[III, i, 1–91] *Set to slave for Prospero, after being shipwrecked on his enchanted island, Prince Ferdinand takes comfort from the sympathy of his beautiful daughter, Miranda:*

There be some sports are painful, and their labour
Delight in them sets off. Some kinds of baseness
Are nobly undergone, and most poor matters
Point to rich ends. This my mean task
Would be as heavy to me as odious, but
The mistress which I serve quickens what's dead,
And makes my labours pleasures. O, she is
Ten times more gentle than her father's crabbed,
And he's composed of harshness. I must remove
Some thousands of these logs and pile them up,
Upon a sore injunction. My sweet mistress
Weeps when she sees me work, and says such baseness
Had never like executor. I forget;
But these sweet thoughts do even refresh my labours,
Most busy lest when I do it.

Enter Miranda, and Prospero at a distance, unseen

MIRANDA

                       Alas, now pray you
Work not so hard. I would the lightning had
Burnt up those logs that you are enjoined to pile!
Pray, set it down and rest you. When this burns,

'Twill weep for having wearied you. My father
Is hard at study. Pray now, rest yourself.
He's safe for these three hours.

FERDINAND

O most dear mistress,
The sun will set before I shall discharge
What I must strive to do.

MIRANDA

If you'll sit down,
I'll bear your logs the while. Pray give me that.
I'll carry it to the pile.

FERDINAND

No, precious creature.
I had rather crack my sinews, break my back,
Than you should such dishonour undergo,
While I sit lazy by.

MIRANDA

It would become me
As well as it does you; and I should do it
With much more ease; for my good will is to it,
And yours it is against.

PROSPERO (*aside*)

Poor worm, thou art infected.
This visitation shows it.

MIRANDA

You look wearily.

FERDINAND

No, noble mistress, 'tis fresh morning with me
When you are by at night. I do beseech you,
Chiefly that I might set it in my prayers,
What is your name?

MIRANDA

                    Miranda. O my father,
I have broke your hest to say so!

FERDINAND

                         Admired Miranda!
Indeed, the top of admiration, worth
What's dearest to the world. Full many a lady
I have eyed with best regard, and many a time
Th'harmony of their tongues hath into bondage
Brought my too diligent ear. For several virtues
Have I liked several women; never any
With so full soul but some defect in her
Did quarrel with the noblest grace she owed,
And put it to the foil. But you, O you,
So perfect and so peerless, are created
Of every creature's best.

MIRANDA

                    I do not know
One of my sex; no woman's face remember,
Save, from my glass, mine own. Nor have I seen
More that I may call men than you, good friend,
And my dear father. How features are abroad,
I am skill-less of; but, by my modesty,
The jewel in my dower, I would not wish
Any companion in the world but you.
Nor can imagination form a shape,
Besides yourself, to like of. But I prattle
Something too wildly, and my father's precepts
I therein do forget.

FERDINAND

               I am, in my condition,

A prince, Miranda; I do think, a king –
I would not so – and would no more endure
This wooden slavery than to suffer
The flesh-fly blow my mouth. Hear my soul speak.
The very instant that I saw you did
My heart fly to your service, there resides
To make me slave to it; and for your sake
Am I this patient log-man.

MIRANDA

                Do you love me?

FERDINAND

O heaven, O earth, bear witness to this sound,
And crown what I profess with kind event,
If I speak true! If hollowly, invert
What best is boded me to mischief! I,
Beyond all limit of what else i'th'world,
Do love, prize, honour you.

MIRANDA

                I am a fool
To weep at what I am glad of.

PROSPERO (*aside*)

                Fair encounter
Of two most rare affections. Heavens rain grace
On that which breeds between 'em.

FERDINAND

                Wherefore weep you?

MIRANDA

At mine unworthiness, that dare not offer
What I desire to give, and much less take
What I shall die to want. But this is trifling;
And all the more it seeks to hide itself,

The bigger bulk it shows. Hence, bashful cunning!
And prompt me, plain and holy innocence.
I am your wife, if you will marry me.
If not, I'll die your maid. To be your fellow
You may deny me, but I'll be your servant
Whether you will or no.

FERDINAND

My mistress, dearest,
And I thus humble ever.

MIRANDA

My husband, then?

FERDINAND

Ay, with a heart as willing
As bondage e'er of freedom. Here's my hand.

MIRANDA

And mine, with my heart in't; and now farewell
Till half an hour hence.

The Two Noble Kinsmen

[II, iii, 1–33] *Enamoured with the prisoner Prince Palamon,
the jailer's daughter reflects on some realities of love. Yet these
will not, she realizes, dissuade her from a desperate course of
action:*

Why should I love this gentleman? 'Tis odds
He never will affect me; I am base,
My Father the mean keeper of his prison,
And he a prince. To marry him is hopeless;
To be his whore is witless. Out upon't!
What pushes are we wenches driven to,
When fifteen once has found us! First, I saw him;
I, seeing, thought he was a goodly man;
He has as much to please a woman in him –
If he please to bestow it so – as ever
These eyes yet looked on. Next, I pitied him,
And so would any young wench, o'my conscience,
That ever dreamed, or vowed her maidenhead
To a young handsome man. Then I loved him,
Extremely loved him, infinitely loved him;
And yet he had a cousin, fair as he too.
But in my heart was Palamon, and there,
Lord, what a coil he keeps! To hear him
Sing in an evening, what a heaven it is!
And yet his songs are sad ones. Fairer spoken

Was never gentleman. When I come in
To bring him water in a morning, first
He bows his noble body, then salutes me, thus:
'Fair, gentle maid, good morrow; may thy goodness
Get thee a happy husband.' Once he kissed me;
I loved my lips the better ten days after –
Would he would do so every day! He grieves much,
And me as much to see his misery.
What should I do, to make him know I love him?
For I would fain enjoy him. Say I ventured
To set him free? What says the law then? Thus much
For law, or kindred! I will do it;
And this night; or tomorrow, he shall love me.

The Phoenix and Turtle

*Phoenix and turtle dove are partners in this extraordinary
poem, a mystic allegory of the married union in which the
principles of endless duration and devoted loyalty are joined.
The phoenix is, of course, the mythical bird which rises new-
born from the ashes of that very fire in which it has been
consumed; the dove an age-old symbol of loving tenderness.
(The poem has been read as a historical allegory too, with
various candidates for the different roles: Queen Elizabeth I as
the phoenix, and the Earl of Essex as the turtle, for example.)
After a funeral attended by the other birds, both are buried
together in this poem, with every appearance of finality – an
end to endless love, or a challenge thrown down to future
lovers?*

Let the bird of loudest lay
On the sole Arabian tree
Herald sad and trumpet be,
To whose sound chaste wings obey.

But thou shrieking harbinger,
Foul precurrer of the fiend,
Augur of the fever's end,
To this troop come thou not near.

From this session interdict
Every fowl of tyrant wing,
Save the eagle, feathered king:
Keep the obsequy so strict.

Let the priest in surplice white,
That defunctive music can,
Be the death-divining swan,
Lest the requiem lack his right.

And thou treble-dated crow,
That thy sable gender mak'st
With the breath thou giv'st and tak'st,
'Mongst our mourners shalt thou go.

Here the anthem doth commence:
Love and constancy is dead,
Phoenix and the turtle fled
In a mutual flame from hence.

So they loved as love in twain
Had the essence but in one;
Two distincts, division none:
Number there in love was slain.

Hearts remote, yet not asunder;
Distance, and no space was seen
'Twixt this turtle and his queen:
But in them it were a wonder.

So between them love did shine
That the turtle saw his right
Flaming in the phoenix' sight;
Either was the other's mine.

Property was thus appalled,
That the self was not the same;
Single nature's double name
Neither two nor one was called.

Reason, in itself confounded,
Saw division grow together,
To themselves yet either neither,
Simple were so well confounded;

That it cried, 'How true a twain
Seemeth this concordant one!
Love hath reason, reason none,
If what parts can so remain.'

Whereupon it made this threne
To the phoenix and the dove,
Co-supremes and stars of love,
As chorus to their tragic scene.

(*threnos*)
Beauty, truth, and rarity,
Grace in all simplicity,
Here enclosed, in cinders lie.

Death is now the phoenix' nest;
And the turtle's loyal breast
To eternity doth rest.

Leaving no posterity:
'Twas not their infirmity,
It was married chastity.

Truth may seem, but cannot be;
Beauty brag, but 'tis not she;
Truth and Beauty buried be.

To this urn let those repair
That are either true or fair;
For these dead birds sigh a prayer.

The Sonnets

[1, 2, 12] *That so many of Shakespeare's sonnets should be addressed to a young man no longer seems as strange (not to say disturbing) as it once did, yet immense question marks still hang over the earlier part of the sequence in particular. Here the poet exhorts the 'fair youth' to prolong his beauty by producing children. 'Love poetry' this surely is, though it's an odd sort of love poetry that urges its recipient to make love with someone else! Hence the suggestion that these sonnets express a 'displaced' homosexual desire:*

From fairest creatures we desire increase,
That thereby beauty's rose might never die,
But as the riper should by time decease,
His tender heir might bear his memory;
But thou, contracted to thine own bright eyes,
Feed'st thy light's flame with self-substantial fuel,
Making a famine where abundance lies,
Thyself thy foe, to thy sweet self too cruel.
Thou that art now the world's fresh ornament
And only herald to the gaudy spring,
Within thine own bud buriest thy content
And, tender churl, mak'st waste in niggarding.
   Pity the world, or else this glutton be,
   To eat the world's due, by the grave and thee.

When forty winters shall besiege thy brow
And dig deep trenches in thy beauty's field,
Thy youth's proud livery, so gazed on now,
Will be a tottered weed of small worth held.
Then being asked where all thy beauty lies,
Where all the treasure of thy lusty days,
To say within thine own deep-sunken eyes
Were an all-eating shame and thriftless praise.
How much more praise deserved thy beauty's use
If thou couldst answer, 'This fair child of mine
Shall sum my count, and make my old excuse,'
Proving his beauty by succession thine.
    This were to be new made when thou art old
    And see thy blood warm when thou feel'st it cold.

When I do count the clock that tells the time
And see the brave day sunk in hideous night,
When I behold the violet past prime
And sable curls all silvered o'er with white,
When lofty trees I see barren of leaves,
Which erst from heat did canopy the herd,
And summer's green all girded up in sheaves
Borne on the bier with white and bristly beard;
Then of thy beauty do I question make
That thou among the wastes of time must go,
Since sweets and beauties do themselves forsake
And die as fast as they see others grow;
    And nothing 'gainst Time's scythe can make defence
    Save breed, to brave him when he takes thee hence.

[18, 19] *But, poetic modesty aside, Shakespeare can suggest another way in which the young man may triumph over time and death – in the immortal greatness of these very sonnets:*

Shall I compare thee to a summer's day?
Thou art more lovely and more temperate.
Rough winds do shake the darling buds of May,
And summer's lease hath all too short a date.
Sometime too hot the eye of heaven shines,
And often is his gold complexion dimmed;
And every fair from fair sometime declines,
By chance or nature's changing course, untrimmed:
But thy eternal summer shall not fade,
Nor lose possession of that fair thou ow'st,
Nor shall Death brag thou wand'rest in his shade
When in eternal lines to time thou grow'st.
   So long as men can breathe or eyes can see,
   So long lives this, and this gives life to thee.

Devouring Time, blunt thou the lion's paws,
And make the earth devour her own sweet brood;
Pluck the keen teeth from the fierce tiger's jaws,
And burn the long-lived phoenix, in her blood;
Make glad and sorry seasons as thou fleet'st,
And do whate'er thou wilt, swift-footed Time,
To the wide world and all her fading sweets.
But I forbid thee one most heinous crime:
O carve not with thy hours my love's fair brow,
Nor draw no lines there with thine antique pen;
Him in thy course untainted do allow
For beauty's pattern to succeeding men.

Yet do thy worst, old Time; despite thy wrong,
My love shall in my verse ever live young.

[20] *This sonnet was long held to be the 'clincher' that saved
England's national poet from the stigma of homosexuality –
though it surely raises as many questions as it resolves:*

A woman's face, with Nature's own hand painted,
Hast thou, the master-mistress of my passion;
A woman's gentle heart, but not acquainted
With shifting change, as is false women's fashion;
An eye more bright than theirs, less false in rolling,
Gilding the object whereupon it gazeth;
A man in hue all hues in his controlling,
Which steals men's eyes and women's souls amazeth.
And for a woman wert thou first created,
Till Nature as she wrought thee fell a-doting,
And by addition me of thee defeated
By adding one thing to my purpose nothing.
  But since she pricked thee out for women's pleasure,
  Mine be thy love, and thy love's use their treasure.

[29, 30] *Just the very knowledge that one is loved, Shakespeare
suggests, can be a great support in times of trouble . . .*

When, in disgrace with Fortune and men's eyes,
I all alone beweep my outcast state,
And trouble deaf heaven with my bootless cries,
And look upon myself and curse my fate,

Wishing me like to one more rich in hope,
Featured like him, like him with friends possessed,
Desiring this man's art, and that man's scope,
With what I most enjoy contented least;
Yet, in these thoughts myself almost despising,
Haply I think on thee, and then my state,
Like to the lark at break of day arising
From sullen earth, sings hymns at heaven's gate;
   For thy sweet love remembered such wealth brings
   That then I scorn to change my state with kings.

When to the sessions of sweet silent thought
I summon up remembrance of things past,
I sigh the lack of many a thing I sought,
And with old woes new wail my dear time's waste;
Then can I drown an eye, unused to flow,
For precious friends hid in death's dateless night,
And weep afresh love's long since cancelled woe,
And moan th'expense of many a vanished sight;
Then can I grieve at grievances foregone,
And heavily from woe to woe tell o'er
The sad account of fore-bemoanèd moan,
Which I new pay as if not paid before.
   But if the while I think on thee, dear friend,
   All losses are restored and sorrows end.

[32] *The young man, he says, should derive similar comfort
from these sonnets, which make up in sincerity for anything
they might lack in art:*

If thou survive my well-contented day
When that churl Death my bones with dust shall
    cover,
And shalt by fortune once more resurvey
These poor rude lines of thy deceasèd lover,
Compare them with the bett'ring of the time,
And though they be outstripped by every pen,
Reserve them for my love, not for their rhyme,
Exceeded by the height of happier men.
O, then vouchsafe me but this loving thought:
'Had my friend's Muse grown with this growing age,
A dearer birth than this his love had brought
To march in ranks of better equipage;
    But since he died, and poets better prove,
    Theirs for their style I'll read, his for his love.'

[33] *Along with strength, however, love may bring vulnerability
– the Youth's unkindnesses can blight the poet's whole
existence:*

Full many a glorious morning have I seen
Flatter the mountain tops with sovereign eye,
Kissing with golden face the meadows green,
Gilding pale streams with heavenly alchemy,

Anon permit the basest clouds to ride
With ugly rack on his celestial face,
And from the forlorn world his visage hide,
Stealing unseen to west with this disgrace.
Even so my sun one early morn did shine
With all-triumphant splendour on my brow;
But, out alack, he was but one hour mine,
The region cloud hath masked him from me now,
  Yet him for this my love no whit disdaineth;
  Suns of the world may stain when heaven's sun
    staineth.

[34] *But signs of real repentance may do much to make
amends:*

Why didst thou promise such a beauteous day
And make me travel forth without my cloak,
To let base clouds o'ertake me in my way,
Hiding thy brav'ry in their rotten smoke?
'Tis not enough that through the cloud thou break
To dry the rain on my storm-beaten face,
For no man well of such a salve can speak
That heals the wound and cures not the disgrace.
Nor can thy shame give physic to my grief;
Though thou repent, yet I have still the loss.
Th' offender's sorrow lends but weak relief
To him that bears the strong offence's cross.
  Ah, but those tears are pearl which thy love sheeds,
  And they are rich and ransom all ill deeds.

[35] So deeply does he love the Youth that Shakespeare can't help continuing to be his advocate, even when he has been the victim of his wrongs:

No more be grieved at that which thou hast done:
Roses have thorns, and silver fountains mud;
Clouds and eclipses stain both moon and sun,
And loathsome canker lives in sweetest bud;
All men make faults, and even I in this,
Authorizing thy trespass with compare,
Myself corrupting, salving thy amiss,
Excusing thy sins more than thy sins are;
For to thy sensual fault I bring in sense –
Thy adverse party is thy advocate –
And 'gainst myself a lawful plea commence.
Such civil war is in my love and hate
   That I an accessary needs must be
   To that sweet thief which sourly robs from me.

[40, 49] The poet has no alternative in his hopeless passion to taking a forgiving line on infidelity – even the theft of his own mistress. What claim has he, after all, on the young man's love?

Take all my loves, my love, yea, take them all;
What hast thou then more than thou hadst before?
No love, my love, that thou mayst true love call;
All mine was thine before thou hadst this more.
Then, if for my love thou my love receivest,
I cannot blame thee for my love thou usest;

But yet be blamed, if thou thy self deceivest
By wilful taste of what thyself refusest.
I do forgive thy robb'ry, gentle thief,
Although thou steal thee all my poverty;
And yet love knows it is a greater grief
To bear love's wrong than hate's known injury.
　　Lascivious grace, in whom all ill well shows,
　　Kill me with spites; yet we must not be foes.

Against that time – if ever that time come –
When I shall see thee frown on my defects,
Whenas thy love hath cast his utmost sum,
Called to that audit by advised respects;
Against that time when thou shalt strangely pass
And scarcely greet me with that sun, thine eye,
When love, converted from the thing it was,
Shall reasons find of settled gravity:
Against that time do I ensconce me here
Within the knowledge of mine own desert,
And this my hand against myself uprear,
To guard the lawful reasons on thy part.
　　To leave poor me thou hast the strength of laws,
　　Since why to love I can allege no cause.

[55, 60, 63] *Confident as a writer, if not as a lover, Shakespeare
renews his promises of poetic immortality:*

Not marble nor the gilded monuments
Of princes shall outlive this powerful rhyme,
But you shall shine more bright in these contents

Than unswept stone, besmeared with sluttish time.
When wasteful war shall statues overturn,
And broils root out the work of masonry,
Nor Mars his sword nor war's quick fire shall burn
The living record of your memory.
'Gainst death and all-oblivious enmity
Shall you pace forth; your praise shall still find room
Even in the eyes of all posterity
That wear this world out to the ending doom.
    So, till the judgement that yourself arise,
    You live in this, and dwell in lovers' eyes.

Like as the waves make towards the pebbled shore,
So do our minutes hasten to their end;
Each changing place with that which goes before,
In sequent toil all forwards do contend.
Nativity, once in the main of light,
Crawls to maturity, wherewith being crowned,
Crooked eclipses 'gainst his glory fight,
And Time that gave doth now his gift confound.
Time doth transfix the flourish set on youth
And delves the parallels in beauty's brow,
Feeds on the rarities of nature's truth,
And nothing stands but for his scythe to mow:
    And yet to times in hope my verse shall stand,
    Praising thy worth, despite his cruel hand.

Against my love shall be as I am now,
With Time's injurious hand crushed and o'erworn;
When hours have drained his blood and filled his brow
With lines and wrinkles, when his youthful morn

Hath travelled on to age's steepy night,
And all those beauties whereof now he's king
Are vanishing or vanished out of sight,
Stealing away the treasure of his spring –
For such a time do I now fortify
Against confounding Age's cruel knife,
That he shall never cut from memory
My sweet love's beauty, though my lover's life.
  His beauty shall in these black lines be seen,
  And they shall live, and he in them still green.

[64, 65] *That grand assurance seems to be faltering:*

When I have seen by Time's fell hand defaced
The rich proud cost of outworn buried age,
When sometime lofty towers I see down-razed,
And brass eternal slave to mortal rage;
When I have seen the hungry ocean gain
Advantage on the kingdom of the shore,
And the firm soil win of the wat'ry main,
Increasing store with loss and loss with store;
When I have seen such interchange of state,
Or state itself confounded to decay,
Ruin hath taught me thus to ruminate –
That Time will come and take my love away.
  This thought is as a death, which cannot choose
  But weep to have that which it fears to lose.

Since brass, nor stone, nor earth, nor boundless sea,
But sad mortality o'ersways their power,
How with this rage shall beauty hold a plea,
Whose action is no stronger than a flower?
O, how shall summer's honey breath hold out
Against the wrackful siege of battering days,
When rocks impregnable are not so stout,
Nor gates of steel so strong, but Time decays?
O, fearful meditation! Where, alack,
Shall Time's best jewel from Time's chest lie hid?
Or what strong hand can hold his swift foot back?
Or who his spoil of beauty can forbid?
    O, none, unless this miracle have might,
    That in black ink my love may still shine bright.

[71, 73] *A bravura exhibition of selflessness: how could such
disinterested devotion fail to make the young man love him
more?*

No longer mourn for me when I am dead
Than you shall hear the surly sullen bell
Give warning to the world that I am fled
From this vile world, with vilest worms to dwell.
Nay, if you read this line, remember not
The hand that writ it, for I love you so
That I in your sweet thoughts would be forgot
If thinking on me then should make you woe.

O, if, I say, you look upon this verse
When I, perhaps, compounded am with clay,
Do not so much as my poor name rehearse,
But let your love even with my life decay;
   Lest the wise world should look into your moan
   And mock you with me after I am gone.

That time of year thou mayst in me behold
When yellow leaves, or none, or few, do hang
Upon those boughs which shake against the cold,
Bare ruined choirs where late the sweet birds sang.
In me thou seest the twilight of such day
As after sunset fadeth in the west,
Which by and by black night doth take away,
Death's second self, that seals up all in rest.
In me thou seest the glowing of such fire
That on the ashes of his youth doth lie,
As the deathbed whereon it must expire,
Consumed with that which it was nourished by.
   This thou perceiv'st, which makes thy love more
     strong,
    To love that well which thou must leave ere long.

[87, 91] *Again, the poet's uneasy recognition that his love
brings as much vulnerability as it does strength:*

Farewell, thou art too dear for my possessing,
And like enough thou know'st thy estimate.
The charter of thy worth gives thee releasing;
My bonds in thee are all determinate.

For how do I hold thee but by thy granting,
And for that riches where is my deserving?
The cause of this fair gift in me is wanting,
And so my patent back again is swerving.
Thyself thou gav'st, thy own worth then not knowing,
Or me, to whom thou gav'st it, else mistaking;
So thy great gift, upon misprision growing,
Comes home again, on better judgement making.
   Thus have I had thee as a dream doth flatter,
   In sleep a king, but waking no such matter.

Some glory in their birth, some in their skill,
Some in their wealth, some in their body's force,
Some in their garments, though newfangled ill,
Some in their hawks and hounds, some in their horse;
And every humour hath his adjunct pleasure,
Wherein it finds a joy above the rest.
But these particulars are not my measure;
All these I better in one general best.
Thy love is better than high birth to me,
Richer than wealth, prouder than garments' costs,
Of more delight than hawks or horses be;
And having thee, of all men's pride I boast –
   Wretched in this alone, that thou mayst take
   All this away and me most wretched make.

[94] Power brings responsibility, Shakespeare says: the Youth should show magnanimity; not to do so would defile his extraordinary beauty:

They that have pow'r to hurt and will do none,
That do not do the thing they most do show,
Who, moving others, are themselves as stone,
Unmovèd, cold, and to temptation slow;
They rightly do inherit heaven's graces
And husband nature's riches from expense;
They are the lords and owners of their faces,
Others but stewards of their excellence.
The summer's flow'r is to the summer sweet,
Though to itself it only live and die;
But if that flow'r with base infection meet,
The basest weed outbraves his dignity:
    For sweetest things turn sourest by their deeds;
    Lilies that fester smell far worse than weeds.

[97, 98] Nature's beauties are as nothing beside those of the young man: the world is wintry and bleak when the poet is parted from his beloved:

How like a winter hath my absence been
From thee, the pleasure of the fleeting year!
What freezings have I felt, what dark days seen –
What old December's bareness everywhere!
And yet this time removed was summer's time,
The teeming autumn, big with rich increase,
Bearing the wanton burden of the prime,

Like widowed wombs after their lords' decease.
Yet this abundant issue seemed to me
But hope of orphans and unfathered fruit;
For summer and his pleasures wait on thee,
And, thou away, the very birds are mute;
　Or, if they sing, 'tis with so dull a cheer
　That leaves look pale, dreading the winter's near.

From you have I been absent in the spring,
When proud-pied April, dressed in all his trim,
Hath put a spirit of youth in everything,
That heavy Saturn laughed and leaped with him;
Yet nor the lays of birds, nor the sweet smell
Of different flowers in odour and in hue,
Could make me any summer's story tell,
Or from their proud lap pluck them where they grew.
Nor did I wonder at the lily's white,
Nor praise the deep vermilion in the rose;
They were but sweet, but figures of delight,
Drawn after you, you pattern of all those.
　Yet seemed it winter still, and, you away,
　As with your shadow I with these did play.

[99] *Such delights as the rest of creation may offer, indeed, by*
rights belong to the Youth – they have been taken from him
by an envious nature:

The forward violet thus did I chide:
'Sweet thief, whence didst thou steal thy sweet that
　　smells,

If not from my love's breath? The purple pride
Which on thy soft cheek for complexion dwells
In my love's veins thou hast too grossly dyed.'
The lily I condemnèd for thy hand;
And buds of marjoram had stol'n thy hair;
The roses fearfully on thorns did stand,
One blushing shame, another white despair;
A third, nor red nor white, had stol'n of both,
And to his robb'ry had annexed thy breath;
But, for his theft, in pride of all his growth
A vengeful canker eat him up to death.
    More flowers I noted, yet I none could see
    But sweet or colour it had stol'n from thee.

[106] *Not just the loveliness of nature now, but all those
beauties praised by the poets of the past, should by rights, says
Shakespeare, belong to his beloved:*

When in the chronicle of wasted time
I see descriptions of the fairest wights,
And beauty making beautiful old rhyme
In praise of ladies dead and lovely knights;
Then, in the blazon of sweet beauty's best,
Of hand, of foot, of lip, of eye, of brow,
I see their antique pen would have expressed
Even such a beauty as you master now.
So all their praises are but prophecies
Of this our time, all you prefiguring;
And, for they looked but with divining eyes,
They had not skill enough your worth to sing:

For we, which now behold these present days,
Have eyes to wonder, but lack tongues to praise.

[109, 110] *On the defensive all of a sudden, the poet suggests
that he may not have behaved as badly as immediately appears
– and besides, whatever his past faults, he has now been
purified in the young man's love:*

O, never say that I was false of heart,
Though absence seemed my flame to qualify.
As easy might I from myself depart
As from my soul, which in thy breast doth lie.
That is my home of love: if I have ranged,
Like him that travels I return again,
Just to the time, not with the time exchanged,
So that myself bring water for my stain.
Never believe, though in my nature reigned
All frailties that besiege all kinds of blood,
That it could so preposterously be stained
To leave for nothing all thy sum of good;
    For nothing this wide universe I call
    Save thou, my rose; in it thou art my all.

Alas, 'tis true, I have gone here and there
And made myself a motley to the view,
Gored mine own thoughts, sold cheap what is most
    dear,
Made old offences of affections new.

Most true it is that I have looked on truth
Askance and strangely; but, by all above,
These blenches gave my heart another youth,
And worse essays proved thee my best of love.
Now all is done, have what shall have no end:
Mine appetite I never more will grind
On newer proof, to try an older friend,
A god in love, to whom I am confined.
    Then give me welcome, next my heaven the best,
    Even to thy pure and most loving breast.

[116] *The classic expression of what love might be – but is it too
idealized ever to be attainable? Shakespeare does get himself
tied into a few logical and grammatical knots in this famous
poem . . .*

Let me not to the marriage of true minds
Admit impediments; love is not love
Which alters when it alteration finds
Or bends with the remover to remove.
O, no, it is an ever-fixèd mark
That looks on tempests and is never shaken;
It is the star to every wandering bark,
Whose worth's unknown, although his height be taken.
Love's not Time's fool, though rosy lips and cheeks
Within his bending sickle's compass come;
Love alters not with his brief hours and weeks,
But bears it out even to the edge of doom.
    If this be error, and upon me proved,
    I never writ, nor no man ever loved.

[127] *Introducing the 'Dark Lady' – for all her darkness, she's still 'fair'.*

In the old age black was not counted fair,
Or, if it were, it bore not beauty's name;
But now is black beauty's successive heir,
And beauty slandered with a bastard shame:
For since each hand hath put on nature's power,
Fairing the foul with art's false borrowed face,
Sweet beauty hath no name, no holy bower,
But is profaned, if not lives in disgrace.
Therefore my mistress' brows are raven black,
Her eyes so suited, and they mourners seem
At such who, not born fair, no beauty lack,
Sland'ring creation with a false esteem.
    Yet so they mourn, becoming of their woe,
    That every tongue says beauty should look so.

[129] *From the rarefied heights of idealized love in Sonnet 116 to the very pit of passion here, a savagely compelling, utterly ignoble animal hunger:*

Th' expense of spirit in a waste of shame
Is lust in action; and, till action, lust
Is perjured, murd'rous, bloody, full of blame,
Savage, extreme, rude, cruel, not to trust;
Enjoyed no sooner but despisèd straight,
Past reason hunted, and no sooner had,
Past reason hated as a swallowed bait
On purpose laid to make the taker mad;

Mad in pursuit, and in possession so,
Had, having, and in quest to have, extreme,
A bliss in proof, and proved, a very woe,
Before, a joy proposed, behind, a dream.
   All this the world well knows; yet none knows well
   To shun the heaven that leads men to this hell.

[130] *This sonnet has been celebrated as a send-up of the sort of hyperbolic imagery associated with verse influenced by the fourteenth-century Italian master, Petrarch, yet coming straight after Sonnet 129 it suggests a somewhat stronger ambivalence:*

My mistress' eyes are nothing like the sun;
Coral is far more red than her lips' red;
If snow be white, why then her breasts are dun;
If hairs be wires, black wires grow on her head.
I have seen roses damasked, red and white,
But no such roses see I in her cheeks;
And in some perfumes is there more delight
Than in the breath that from my mistress reeks.
I love to hear her speak; yet well I know
That music hath a far more pleasing sound.
I grant I never saw a goddess go;
My mistress, when she walks, treads on the ground.
   And yet by heaven, I think my love as rare
   As any she belied with false compare.

[144, 147] *The Dark Lady of the Sonnets is one corner of an eternal (indeed, infernal) triangle, which is nowhere more powerfully presented than it is in these two poems. The corruption, disease and foulness for which she stands may blast the beauty and virtue of the Youth, not only symbolically but (if she really 'fires him out' with syphilis) all too literally:*

Two loves I have, of comfort and despair,
Which like two spirits do suggest me still;
The better angel is a man right fair,
The worser spirit a woman coloured ill.
To win me soon to hell, my female evil
Tempteth my better angel from my side,
And would corrupt my saint to be a devil,
Wooing his purity with her foul pride.
And whether that my angel be turned fiend
Suspect I may, yet not directly tell;
But being both from me, both to each friend,
I guess one angel in another's hell.
    Yet this shall I ne'er know, but live in doubt
    Till my bad angel fire my good one out.

My love is as a fever, longing still
For that which longer nurseth the disease,
Feeding on that which doth preserve the ill,
Th'uncertain sickly appetite to please.
My reason, the physician to my love,
Angry that his prescriptions are not kept,
Hath left me, and I desperate now approve
Desire is death, which physic did except.

Past cure I am, now reason is past care,
And frantic-mad with evermore unrest;
My thoughts and my discourse as madmen's are,
At random from the truth, vainly expressed:
    For I have sworn thee fair, and thought thee bright,
    Who art as black as hell, as dark as night.

A Lover's Complaint

[1–56] *Neglected for centuries because of its rhetorical*
elaboration and self-conscious cleverness, A Lover's
Complaint is being rediscovered by a readership appreciative
of its brilliant inventiveness – and a certain understated
sympathy. Out in the fields one day, the poet overhears the
complaint of a country 'maid' (in fact, a maid no more), whom
he sees tearing letters and tossing love tokens into a nearby
stream. As she has learned to her cost, words of love are not
necessarily true, and the most passionate protestations of love
are by no means always the most sincere:

From off a hill whose concave womb re-worded
A plaintful story from a sist'ring vale,
My spirits t'attend this double voice accorded,
And down I laid to list the sad-tuned tale;
Ere long espied a fickle maid full pale,
Tearing of papers, breaking rings a-twain,
Storming her world with sorrow's wind and rain.

Upon her head a platted hive of straw,
Which fortified her visage from the sun,
Whereon the thought might think sometime it saw
The carcass of a beauty spent and done.
Time had not scythèd all that youth begun,

Nor youth all quit; but spite of heaven's fell rage,
Some beauty peeped through lattice of seared age.

Oft did she heave her napkin to her eyne,
Which on it had conceited characters,
Laund'ring the silken figures in the brine
That seasoned woe had pelleted in tears,
And often reading what contents it bears;
As often shrieking undistinguished woe,
In clamours of all size, both high and low.

Sometimes her levelled eyes their carriage ride,
As they did batt'ry to the spheres intend;
Sometime diverted their poor balls are tied
To th'orbèd earth; sometimes they do extend
Their view right on; anon their gazes lend
To every place at once, and nowhere fixed,
The mind and sight distractedly commixed.

Her hair, nor loose nor tied in formal plat,
Proclaimed in her a careless hand of pride,
For some, untucked, descended her sheaved hat,
Hanging her pale and pinèd cheek beside;
Some in her threaden fillet still did bide
And, true to bondage, would not break from thence,
Though slackly braided in loose negligence.

A thousand favours from a maund she drew,
Of amber, crystal, and of bedded jet,
Which one by one she in a river threw,
Upon whose weeping margent she was set,

Like usury, applying wet to wet,
Or monarch's hands that lets not bounty fall
Where want cries some but where excess begs all.

Of folded schedules had she many a one
Which she perused, sighed, tore, and gave the flood;
Cracked many a ring of posied gold and bone,
Bidding them find their sepulchres in mud;
Found yet more letters sadly penned in blood,
With sleided silk feat and affectedly
Enswathed and sealed to curious secrecy.

These often bathed she in her fluxive eyes,
And often kissed, and often gave to tear;
Cried 'O false blood, thou register of lies,
What unapprovèd witness dost thou bear!
Ink would have seemed more black and damnèd here!'
This said, in top of rage the lines she rents,
Big discontents so breaking their contents.

[288–329] *An old man herding cattle comes to the girl's
assistance and the poet hears her tell him the sad story of how
– proof against good looks, gentle birth and fine flatteries – she
was finally betrayed by her compassion:*

'O father, what a hell of witchcraft lies
In the small orb of one particular tear!
But with the inundation of the eyes
What rocky heart to water will not wear?
What breast so cold that is not warmèd here?

O cleft effect! cold modesty, hot wrath,
Both fire from hence and chill extincture hath.

'For, lo, his passion, but an art of craft,
Even there resolved my reason into tears;
There my white stole of chastity I daffed,
Shook off my sober guards and civil fears,
Appear to him as he to me appears –
All melting; though our drops this diff'rence bore:
His poisoned me, and mine did him restore.

'In him a plenitude of subtle matter,
Applied to cautels, all strange forms receives,
Of burning blushes, or of weeping water,
Or sounding paleness; and he takes and leaves,
In either's aptness, as it best deceives,
To blush at speeches rank, to weep at woes,
Or to turn white and sound at tragic shows;

'That not a heart which in his level came
Could 'scape the hail of his all-hurting aim,
Showing fair nature is both kind and tame;
And, veiled in them, did win whom he would maim.
Against the thing he sought he would exclaim:
When he most burned in heart-wished luxury,
He preached pure maid and praised cold chastity.

'Thus merely with the garment of a grace
The naked and concealèd fiend he covered;
That th'unexperient gave the tempter place,
Which, like a cherubin, above them hovered.

Who, young and simple, would not be so lovered?
Ay me! I fell; and yet do question make
What I should do again for such a sake.

'O, that infected moisture of his eye,
O, that false fire which in his cheek so glowed,
O, that forced thunder from his heart did fly,
O, that sad breath his spongy lungs bestowed,
O, all that borrowed motion, seeming owed,
Would yet again betray the fore-betrayed
And new pervert a reconcilèd maid.'

Venus and Adonis

*In another undeservedly neglected narrative poem, a famous
classical myth takes on a quality of erotic farce. [1–216] The
love goddess's advances are spurned by the beautiful – but
chaste – Adonis:*

Even as the sun with purple-coloured face
Had ta'en his last leave of the weeping morn,
Rose-cheeked Adonis hied him to the chase.
Hunting he loved, but love he laughed to scorn.
   Sick-thoughted Venus makes amain unto him,
   And like a bold-faced suitor 'gins to woo him.

'Thrice fairer than myself,' thus she began,
'The field's chief flower, sweet above compare,
Stain to all nymphs, more lovely than a man,
More white and red than doves or roses are,
   Nature that made thee, with herself at strife,
   Saith that the world hath ending with thy life.

'Vouchsafe, thou wonder, to alight thy steed,
And rein his proud head to the saddle-bow.
If thou wilt deign this favour, for thy meed
A thousand honey secrets shalt thou know.
   Here come and sit, where never serpent hisses
   And being set, I'll smother thee with kisses.

'And yet not cloy thy lips with loathed satiety,
But rather famish them amid their plenty,
Making them red and pale with fresh variety –
Ten kisses short as one, one long as twenty.
    A summer's day will seem an hour but short,
    Being wasted in such time-beguiling sport.'

With this she seizeth on his sweating palm,
The precedent of pith and livelihood,
And trembling in her passion, calls it balm,
Earth's sovereign salve to do a goddess good.
    Being so enraged, desire doth lend her force
    Courageously to pluck him from his horse.

Over one arm the lusty courser's rein,
Under her other was the tender boy,
Who blushed and pouted in a dull disdain,
With leaden appetite, unapt to toy;
    She red and hot as coals of glowing fire,
    He red for shame, but frosty in desire.

The studded bridle on a ragged bough
Nimbly she fastens – O, how quick is love!
The steed is stallèd up, and even now
To tie the rider she begins to prove.
    Backward she pushed him, as she would be thrust,
    And governed him in strength, though not in lust.

So soon was she along, as he was down,
Each leaning on their elbows and their hips.
Now doth she stroke his cheek, now doth he frown
And 'gins to chide; but soon she stops his lips,
    And kissing speaks, with lustful language broken,
    'If thou wilt chide, thy lips shall never open.'

He burns with bashful shame; she with her tears
Doth quench the maiden burning of his cheeks.
Then with her windy sighs and golden hairs
To fan and blow them dry again she seeks.
    He saith she is immodest, blames her miss;
    What follows more she murders with a kiss.

Even as an empty eagle, sharp by fast,
Tires with her beak on feathers, flesh and bone,
Shaking her wings, devouring all in haste,
Till either gorge be stuffed or prey be gone –
    Even so she kissed his brow, his cheek, his chin,
    And where she ends she doth anew begin.

Forced to content, but never to obey,
Panting he lies and breatheth in her face.
She feedeth on the steam as on a prey,
And calls it heavenly moisture, air of grace,
    Wishing her cheeks were gardens full of flowers,
    So they were dewed with such distilling showers.

Look how a bird lies tangled in a net,
So fast'ned in her arms Adonis lies.
Pure shame and awed resistance made him fret,
Which bred more beauty in his angry eyes.
    Rain added to a river that is rank
    Perforce will force it overflow the bank.

Still she entreats, and prettily entreats,
For to a pretty ear she tunes her tale.
Still is he sullen, still he low'rs and frets,
'Twixt crimson shame and anger ashy-pale.
    Being red, she loves him best, and being white,
    Her best is bettered with a more delight.

Look how he can, she cannot choose but love;
And by her fair immortal hand she swears
From his soft bosom never to remove
Till he take truce with her contending tears,
    Which long have rained, making her cheeks all wet;
    And one sweet kiss shall pay this countless debt.

Upon this promise did he raise his chin,
Like a divedapper peering through a wave,
Who, being looked on, ducks as quickly in.
So offers he to give what she did crave;
    But when her lips were ready for his pay,
    He winks, and turns his lips another way.

Never did passenger in summer's heat
More thirst for drink than she for this good turn.
Her help she sees, but help she cannot get;
She bathes in water, yet her fire must burn.
'O, pity,' 'gan she cry, 'flint-hearted boy!
'Tis but a kiss I beg – why art thou coy?

'I have been wooed, as I entreat thee now,
Even by the stern and direful god of war,
Whose sinewy neck in battle ne'er did bow,
Who conquers where he comes in every jar;
    Yet hath he been my captive and my slave,
    And begged for that which thou unasked shalt have.

'Over my altars hath he hung his lance,
His batt'red shield, his uncontrollèd crest,
And for my sake hath learned to sport and dance,
To toy, to wanton, dally, smile and jest,
    Scorning his churlish drum and ensign red,
    Making my arms his field, his tent my bed.

'Thus he that overruled I overs   wayed,
Leading him prisoner in a red-rose chain;
Strong-tempered steel his stronger strength obeyèd;
Yet was he servile to my coy disdain.
    O, be not proud, nor brag not of thy might,
    For mast'ring her that foiled the god of fight!

'Touch but my lips with those fair lips of thine –
Though mine be not so fair, yet are they red –
The kiss shall be thine own as well as mine.
What seest thou in the ground? hold up thy head,
    Look in mine eyeballs, there thy beauty lies,
    Then why not lips on lips, since eyes in eyes?

'Art thou ashamed to kiss? Then wink again,
And I will wink – so shall the day seem night.
Love keeps his revels where there are but twain.
Be bold to play, our sport is not in sight.
    These blue-veined violets whereon we lean
    Never can blab, nor know not what we mean.

'The tender spring upon thy tempting lip
Shows thee unripe; yet mayst thou well be tasted:
Make use of time, let not advantage slip;
Beauty within itself should not be wasted.
    Fair flowers that are not gathered in their prime
    Rot, and consume themselves in little time.

'Were I hard-favoured, foul, or wrinkled old,
Ill-nurtured, crooked, churlish, harsh in voice,
O'erworn, despisèd, rheumatic and cold,
Thick-sighted, barren, lean, and lacking juice,
    Then mightst thou pause, for then I were not for thee;
    But having no defects, why dost abhor me?

'Thou canst not see one wrinkle in my brow;
Mine eyes are grey and bright, and quick in turning;
My beauty as the spring doth yearly grow,
My flesh is soft and plump, my marrow burning;
    My smooth moist hand, were it with thy hand felt,
    Would in thy palm dissolve or seem to melt.

'Bid me discourse, I will enchant thine ear,
Or like a fairy trip upon the green,
Or, like a nymph, with long dishevelled hair,
Dance on the sands, and yet no footing seen.
    Love is a spirit all compact of fire,
    Not gross to sink, but light, and will aspire.

'Witness this primrose bank whereon I lie;
These forceless flowers like sturdy trees support me.
Two strengthless doves will draw me through the sky
From morn till night, even where I list to sport me.
    Is love so light, sweet boy, and may it be
    That thou should think it heavy unto thee?

'Is thine own heart to thine own face affected?
Can thy right hand seize love upon thy left?
Then woo thyself, be of thyself rejected;
Steal thine own freedom, and complain on theft.
    Narcissus so himself himself forsook.
    And died to kiss his shadow in the brook.

'Torches are made to light, jewels to wear,
Dainties to taste, fresh beauty for the use,
Herbs for their smell, and sappy plants to bear.
Things growing to themselves are growth's abuse.
Seeds spring from seeds and beauty breedeth beauty.
Thou wast begot; to get it is thy duty.

'Upon the earth's increase why shouldst thou feed
Unless the earth with thy increase be fed?
By law of nature thou art bound to breed,
That thine may live when thou thyself art dead;
    And so, in spite of death, thou dost survive,
    In that thy likeness still is left alive.'

By this, the lovesick queen began to sweat,
For where they lay the shadow had forsook them,
And Titan, tirèd in the mid-day heat,
With burning eye did hotly overlook them,
    Wishing Adonis had his team to guide,
    So he were like him, and by Venus' side.

And now Adonis, with a lazy sprite,
And with a heavy, dark, disliking eye,
His low'ring brows o'erwhelming his fair sight,
Like misty vapours when they blot the sky,
    Souring his cheeks, cries, 'Fie, no more of love!
    The sun doth burn my face – I must remove.'

'Ay me,' quoth Venus, 'young, and so unkind!
What bare excuses mak'st thou to be gone!
I'll sigh celestial breath, whose gentle wind
Shall cool the heat of this descending sun;
    I'll make a shadow for thee of my hairs;
    If they burn too, I'll quench them with my tears.

'The sun that shines from heaven shines but warm,
And lo, I lie between that sun and thee;
The heat I have from thence doth little harm,
Thine eye darts forth the fire that burneth me;
    And were I not immortal, life were done
    Between this heavenly and earthly sun.

'Art thou obdurate, flinty, hard as steel?
Nay, more than flint, for stone at rain relenteth.
Art thou a woman's son, and canst not feel
What 'tis to love, how love tormenteth?
    O, had thy mother borne so hard a mind,
    She had not brought forth thee, but died unkind.

'What am I that thou shouldst contemn me this?
Or, what great danger dwells upon my suit?
What were thy lips the worse for one poor kiss?
Speak, fair; but speak fair words or else be mute.
    Give me one kiss, I'll give it thee again,
    And one for interest, if thou wilt have twain.

'Fie, lifeless picture, cold and senseless stone,
Well painted idol, image dull and dead,
Statue contenting but the eye alone,
Thing like a man, but of no woman bred!
    Thou art no man, though of a man's complexion,
    For men will kiss even by their own direction.'

[229–40] *Her imprisoning embrace, she assures him, will
be no irksome confinement but a spell in a veritable soft-porn
paradise.*

'Fondling,' she saith, 'since I have hemmed thee here
Within the circuit of this ivory pale,
I'll be a park, and thou shalt be my deer:
Feed where thou wilt, on mountain or in dale;
    Graze on my lips; and if those hills be dry,
    Stray lower, where the pleasant fountains lie.

'Within this limit is relief enough,
Sweet bottom-grass, and high delightful plain,
Round rising hillocks, brakes obscure and rough,
To shelter thee from tempest and from rain.
    Then be my deer, since I am such a park.
    No dog shall rouse thee, though a thousand bark.'

[463–504] *When she faints clean away before his angry glance, Adonis fears she is dead and embraces her in a panic. She awakens, entranced, to find herself in his arms:*

And at his look she flatly falleth down,
For looks kill love, and love by looks reviveth,
A smile recures the wounding of a frown.
But blessèd bankrupt that by love so thriveth!
    The silly boy, believing she is dead,
    Claps her pale cheek till clapping makes it red,

And all amazed brake off his late intent,
For sharply he did think to reprehend her,
Which cunning love did wittily prevent.
Fair fall the wit that can so well defend her!
    For on the grass she lies as she were slain,
    Till his breath breatheth life in her again.

He wrings her nose, he strikes her on the cheeks,
He bends her finger, holds her pulses hard,
He chafes her lips, a thousand ways he seeks
To mend the hurt that his unkindness marred;
    He kisses her; and she, by her good will,
    Will never rise, so he will kiss her still.

The night of sorrow now is turned to day:
Her two blue windows faintly she upheaveth,
Like the fair sun, when in his fresh array
He cheers the morn, and all the earth relieveth;
    And as the bright sun glorifies the sky,
    So is her face illumined with her eye;

Whose beams upon his hairless face are fixed,
As if from thence they borrowèd all their shine.
Were never four such lamps together mixed,
Had not his clouded with his brows' repine;
    But hers, which through the crystal tears gave light,
    Shone like the moon in water seen by night.

'O, where am I?' quoth she; 'in earth or heaven,
Or in the ocean drenched, or in the fire?
What hour is this? or morn or weary even?
Do I delight to die, or life desire?
    But now I lived, and life was death's annoy;
    But now I died, and death was lively joy.

'O! thou didst kill me; kill me once again.
Thy eyes' shrewd tutor, that hard heart of thine,
Hath taught them scornful tricks, and such disdain
That they have murdered this poor heart of mine;
    And these mine eyes, true leaders to their queen,
    But for thy piteous lips no more had seen.

[595–612] *Learning that he hopes to go hunting after boar,
Venus throws her arms round his neck in terror that he might
be hurt. They sink to the ground, 'he on her belly . . . she on her
back':*

Now is she in the very lists of love,
Her champion mounted for the hot encounter.
All is imaginary she doth prove;
He will not manage her, although he mount her;

That worse than Tantalus' is her annoy,
To clip Elysium and to lack her joy.

Even so poor birds, deceived with painted grapes,
Do surfeit by the eye and pine the maw;
Even so she languisheth in her mishaps
As those poor birds that helpless berries saw.
    The warm effects which she in him finds missing
    She seeks to kindle with continual kissing.

But all in vain, good queen, it will not be,
She hath assayed as much as may be proved:
Her pleading hath deserved a greater fee;
She's Love, she loves, and yet she is not loved.
    'Fie, fie,' he says, 'you crush me; let me go;
    You have no reason to withhold me so.'

[793–804] *Adonis remonstrates with his persecutress, drawing himself up to his highest moral tone:*

'Call it not love, for Love to heaven is fled
Since sweating Lust on earth usurped his name;
Under whose simple semblance he hath fed
Upon fresh beauty, blotting it with blame;
    Which the hot tyrant stains and soon bereaves,
    As caterpillars do the tender leaves.

'Love comforteth like sunshine after rain,
But Lust's effect is tempest after sun.
Love's gentle spring doth always fresh remain;
Lust's winter comes ere summer half be done.
    Love surfeits not, Lust like a glutton dies;
    Love is all truth, Lust full of forgèd lies.

[1135–64] *Having finally freed himself from the goddess's
attentions, Adonis has gone hunting as planned. He has found
a boar, just as he hoped – but it has killed him, just as Venus
feared. Full of frustration and bitterness, she stands over his
bleeding, never-to-be-enjoyed body. She will set a curse on
Love, she says, from that time forth:*

'Since thou art dead, lo, here I prophesy
Sorrow on love hereafter shall attend.
It shall be waited on with jealousy,
Find sweet beginning but unsavoury end,
    Ne'er settled equally, but high or low,
    That all love's pleasure shall not match his woe.

'It shall be fickle, false and full of fraud;
Bud, and be blasted, in a breathing while,
The bottom poison, and the top o'erstrawed
With sweets that shall the truest sight beguile.
    The strongest body shall it make most weak,
    Strike the wise dumb, and teach the fool to speak.

'It shall be sparing, and too full of riot,
Teaching decrepit age to tread the measures;
The staring ruffian shall it keep in quiet,
Pluck down the rich, enrich the poor with treasures;
    It shall be raging-mad, and silly-mild,
    Make the young old, the old become a child.

'It shall suspect where is no cause of fear;
It shall not fear where it should most mistrust;
It shall be merciful, and too severe,
And most deceiving when it seems most just;
    Perverse it shall be where it shows most toward,
    Put fear to valour, courage to the coward.

'It shall be cause of war and dire events
And set dissension 'twixt the son and sire,
Subject and servile to all discontents,
As dry combustious matter is to fire.
    Sith in his prime Death doth my love destroy,
    They that love best their loves shall not enjoy.'

Index of First Lines